THE FOUR
LIVING
CREATURES

Entering God's Kingdom
in the Age of Terror

PATRICIA BAIRD CLARK

Copyright © 2010 by Patricia Baird Clark
All Rights Reserved
www.hispresenceonline.org

Five Stones Publishing
is a division of
The International Localization Network
Easton Kansas 66202 * Randy2905@gmail.com

ISBN: 978-1-935018-19-3

Printed in the United States of America

This book is dedicated to the One who opened the Scriptures to me...
The Lord Jesus Christ

Acknowledgements

I would like to give special thanks to Dr. Larry Stanfield for his work in editing this manuscript. When he first saw it, it was like a bare-bones Bible study with long, boring details regarding the research behind each verse. Larry wisely suggested I shorten some of the research details and give more illustrations and spiritual explanations to clarify my spiritual interpretations. The result was a very different book that is much more understandable and interesting to read.

I also want to express my gratitude to Brenda Wilkinson, my dear sister in the Lord, whose encouragement and prophetic gifting enabled me to persevere through the many challenges related to the Ezekiel study that resulted in not only the writing of this book but also my own deeper walk with God.

And lastly, I am deeply indebted to those Christian scholars of the past whose writings have enabled me, a person of much lesser education and intellect, to study the Word of God in greater depth.

Table of Contents

Introduction

From my earliest years as a student of the Bible, I have been fascinated by the four living creatures. I had not the slightest idea what they symbolized, but I enjoyed reading about them and wondering what they could possibly mean. Finally in 1999, the Lord led me to do an in-depth study of them using a good concordance, a Hebrew lexicon, principles of allegory and a lot of prayer. After about a year of study, I set them aside and delved into some other studies, but returned to them three more times. Each time through, their message became clearer until I knew that God had laid out before me a great message for the church of the end times.

Since completing that study, I have done many other studies similar to it in that I have used the same study methods and studied large blocks of scripture...several consecutive chapters at a time, verse by verse...in the same way the four living creatures were studied. To my amazement, I always find the same truths I found in the four living creatures. I can't get away from this message even if I want to because it is everywhere. I'm beginning to believe the message of the end times and the return of Christ is under the surface in almost every chapter of the Bible!

The Lord indicated it was not yet time for these truths to be revealed, so I placed each study "on the shelf" waiting for the time they could become books. The particulars about the end times needed to be withheld until such a time as they were needed. To know these things before the time could have caused some people to fall into error by trying to enter into something before it was time. Our loving Father knew just how to present these end time truths in such a way that they could only be understood when the time was right. The Holy Spirit had to open these passages and certain tools had to be prepared beforehand in order to facilitate the study.

There has been a lot of conjecture about the events of the end times. Some have claimed to have all the details worked out and some have even predicted the exact time of the Lord's return. We have anticipated there would be a catching up. Many people have believed our bodies would literally fly off the earth at a certain time leaving vehicles unmanned and unsaved loved ones agonizing over our disappearance. We have argued over whether this catching up (or Rapture as some have called it) would happen before, during or after the Great Tribulation. The four living creatures will show us exactly how we are going to be caught up. I can tell you right now that we will not leave our automobiles and airplanes unmanned, and our loved ones will still be able to find us.

Very soon we are going to see God moving in some of the ways revealed in the four living creatures. How do I know this? There are two reasons. The first is because he told me to get busy and publish this book. I completed the first edition of it in 2002 but God would not permit me to publish it at that time. The fact that he said to publish it now says to me that people will soon be experiencing many of the things revealed in the four living creatures. Because these things have never before been experienced, they won't understand what is happening to them. When that occurs, the truths revealed here will be waiting to clarify their experience for them. This book will enable them to learn to see this message in the scriptures for themselves. They will understand how to cooperate with God to more quickly enter into the place he has prepared for his true church in the end times. We are indeed blessed to know the Lord Jesus Christ and to have been chosen to live at this time in history!

The second reason I know it is time for this book to go forward is that the events rapidly taking place in our nation and the world indicate that civilization as we know it is about to come to an end. The stage is being set for the takeover of the Antichrist and the New World Order. We are going to desperately need the information laid out in the pages of this book.

In order to enter the place God has prepared for us, we must learn to walk in holiness. Our character must become like the character of Christ. This is a process that will not happen overnight. God has been preparing certain persons to minister to his faithful church in these ends times. These persons will minister with an anointing the likes of which has not been seen since Christ walked on earth 2000 years ago. These ministers will help the church come up to the place of holiness that will enable them to enter into the kingdom of God even as they are here on earth.

Entering fully into the "measure of the stature of the fullness of Christ" where Ezekiel's visions eventually lead will require, among other things, a deep study of God's word. Certain tools had to be prepared to enable us to study in such depth.

There are six tools I have found to be absolutely essential for the depth of study required to remove the seals from these passages. These tools are: (1) *The New Strong's Expanded Exhaustive Concordance of the Bible*, (2) *The Interpreting Dictionary of Scripture Proper Names*, (3) *Gesenius' Hebrew-Chaldee Lexicon to the Old Testament*, (4) *Number in Scripture* by E. W. Bullinger, (5) *Types in Genesis* by Andrew Jukes and (6) a good English language dictionary.

Strong's concordance will give us the exact meaning of the words in Hebrew. It is important to trace the words back through all their derivatives because much information will be revealed there. When more than one Hebrew word can be translated as one certain English word, we need to research all the words to understand why the Holy Spirit chose this particular word. For example, there are five different Hebrew words that can be translated "visions." To understand why the particular word, *mar'ah*, was chosen for this passage, we need to see how it is different from all the other words. Our research reveals that *mar'ah* is the only Hebrew word for visions that means "a mirror," "a looking glass." This is an important understanding for finding the hidden meaning of this passage.

In addition to the concordances, we need Gesenius' lexicon to give us a deeper and more thorough understanding of the original languages of the Old Testament.

Bullinger's book on numbers will reveal the spiritual meaning of numbers. In this kind of revelatory study, we are not interested in the number's numerical value but in the spiritual meaning of the number based on its usage throughout Scripture. Bullinger has researched each number in great detail giving us marvelous insights into their spiritual meaning. The number four is important in this passage and Bullinger's book contains twelve pages on this number alone. This man's research is thorough and has been indispensible to me in opening the spiritual meaning of this difficult Ezekiel passage.

Andrew Juke's book, *Types in Genesis*, will provide allegorical insights that will unlock hidden meanings. Allegory and parable are both found many places in Scripture. There may be some confusion as to the difference between a parable and an allegory since both employ story and metaphor to convey abstract meaning. Generally speaking a parable is shorter than an allegory and relates only one concept. Allegory, being longer, is used to convey several concepts. Ezekiel 1 is an allegory filled with metaphor that conveys many abstract truths reserved for the church of the end times.

It would be correct to say that a parable is a short form of allegory. Jesus used parables unceasingly when speaking to the multitudes according to Matt. 13:34. "All these things spake Jesus unto the multitude in parables; and without a parable spake he not unto them." He used parables to teach about the kingdom of God. Deep kingdom principles were contained in parables and only those whose hearts were prepared could understand them. As we study the four living creatures, we will find that allegory is an extremely important principle for the church of the end times to understand and use.

The last tool on our list is a good English language dictionary. I use a modern edition as well as the 1828 edition. There are times in my studies when a passage is not opening up for me because I am assuming I know the English definition of the word when in reality I do not. Once I find the exact definition in the dictionary, it is sometimes the key for unlocking the passage.

Now that we understand our study of Ezekiel's visions will be about the end times, that secrets reserved for these last days are revealed here and we know the tools we will be using, it is time to begin our study. We will see here things never before seen by the church—things prepared before the foundations of the world to bring God's people through the devastations of biological and chemical warfare and even nuclear attacks while propelling them into the coming age of the kingdom. The truths revealed here are built upon a solid foundation of biblical truth as revealed in the Scriptures and taught by learned teachers down through the ages.

Chapter One
Signs of the Times

The Vision

    Pastor Bob and his wife were just finishing up at the church for the day when one of their new converts, a young woman named Sue Anne, knocked on the office door. She seemed excited and said that God had told her to come to the church and ask Bob to pray for her with the laying on of hands.

    As the young pastor and his wife prayed for Sue Anne, she suddenly dropped to the floor under the power of the Holy Spirit. It was obvious from things she would mutter and the movement of her eyes that she was having a great vision. The pastor's wife quickly set up a tape recorder to ensure that no details of Sue Anne's account would be forgotten. The following is what was recorded that day in 1971. Surely the time for these events is very near.

> Sue Anne: Please pray for me again; I want to go back to where I was.
>
> Bob: No, you cannot go back. The Lord won't let you go back.
>
> Sue Anne: Please, Bob, I want to go back to where I was.
>
> Bob: No, you can't go back. What did you see?
>
> Sue Anne: I was there in the end times, but I wasn't the only one there. There were other people there...people I know. The earth was brown. Everything was brown. The sky was brown. The trees were brown. They looked like they were burnt but they hadn't really burned. I don't understand. The air was dirty and it was real thick. It was hard to breathe. Demons were everywhere—funny looking little things. You could see them. They were hanging onto the buildings and onto the people. We were white. We were absolutely perfect. We didn't look

old. We looked just like we do now only we were perfect. The people would look at us and burn up. It seemed so cruel. I saw heaven and God was in heaven. I went through three rooms and God was in the third room. It must have been like the tabernacle. I've never seen one but that's what it must have been.

Bob: What did God look like?

Sue Anne: (Long pause while groping for words.) He looks like love. God looks like love. God wasn't alone. There were other people in the room with him but they didn't look like us. I don't know how to describe it but they had this round shape.

Bob: It must have been their spiritual bodies.

Sue Anne: God said to tell you that these people who were perfect were going to have more power than the world has ever seen.

Next in the vision she was shown hell which was a terrifying experience causing her to cry. She said there were a tremendous number of people in hell. There were so many who were not going to go to heaven. She said those who do go to heaven were a great minority. (I was unable to transcribe this part about hell because of damage to the tape rendering it unintelligible.)

* * * * * * * * * * * * * *

Pastor Bob was my brother. I heard the tape shortly after it was recorded and transcribed it as seen here. I include it here because it is an illustration of many things that will be revealed in our study of the four living creatures.

If you are interested in God's plans for his people in the end times, this book is for you. If you would like to be one of the people Sue Anne saw who was absolutely perfect and had more power than the world has ever seen, this book is for you. However, I want to add this caveat, "Many are called, but few are chosen." If you are not willing to allow your life to be crucified with Christ, if you are not willing to give up all worldly desires at the direction of the Holy Spirit, then you will never come to this place in God. Conversely, if you are totally in love with Jesus and willing to forsake all for him, then he will bring you into a great and mighty ministry such as the world has never seen.

The four living creatures of Ezekiel have fascinated God's people down through the ages—such mystery!—creatures with four faces, four wings, wheels within wheels, burning coals of fire and flashes of lightning! Surely these creatures that comprise two entire chapters of Ezekiel must be very important, but who are they and what do they mean?

In ages past great men and women of God have diligently studied and prayed over these verses only to find the true revelation could not be ascertained. This is because God would not allow anyone to understand these passages until the appropriate time determined by him had arrived. That time is now!

If the secrets contained in these verses had been brought forth before their time, people would have misused them. The revelation of the four living creatures contains information to be used only by the Church of the end times. These revelations will sustain us through the turbulent events at the end of this age and propel us into the coming age of the kingdom.

The passing of this age and the establishing of the next could be compared to the meeting of two huge air masses. When a cold front butts up against a warm front, the air becomes turbulent resulting in severe storms and even tornadoes. The events soon to engulf this nation and the entire world will be marked by wild disorder and violent agitation that will shake every society and every institution to the core. Only those things rooted and grounded in Jesus Christ will remain standing.

Just recently we have seen a plunge in world money markets with multitudes losing most if not all of their life savings. The value of the dollar is falling. We have a new class of the homeless as many have lost their homes due to financial problems or severe weather disasters. Our government has been taking over banks and dictating to corporations what they can and cannot do. Freedom of speech is being threatened as our government tries to shun conservative TV stations and monitor talk radio all in the name of "fairness." The validity of our

Constitution is daily being questioned. For those with eyes to see, the move forward toward a One World Government is accelerating at incredible speed. Many attempts are being made to lower our standard of living and bring us down to the level of a third world nation. All the natural things we have trusted in for our security are being removed.

We may be on the very brink of the collapse of civilization as we have known it. Many fear that the end of the world is near. Not only do many Christians believe this, but even secular reporters are taking note as seen in the following headlines:

> An Associated Press writer asks, "Is everything spinning out of control?" A Wall Street Journal headline read, "Millennium Fever: Prophets Proliferate, The End is Near." A New York Times book review began, "Some 50 million Americans share a belief that these are the last days." Even the Chicago Tribune ran a front-page story about the end times in a recent Sunday edition.

> British journalist Malcolm Muggeridge suggested, "The basic condition for a civilization is that there should be law and order. Obviously this is coming to an end. The world is falling into chaos, even perhaps especially our western world... There are many other symptoms. The excessive interest in eroticism is characteristic of the end of a civilization because it really means a growing impotence, and fear of impotence. Then the excessive need for excitement, vicarious excitement, which of course the games provided for the Romans and which television provides for our population. Even the enormously complicated structure of taxation and administration is a symptom of the end of the civilization. Above all, there is this truly terrible thing which afflicts materialist societies - boredom, an excessive boredom which I note on every hand. (Bilson)

A biblical timetable would indicate we are approaching the end of the church age and the beginning of the millennial reign of Christ on earth. If a day is as a thousand years and a thousand years are as a day, with four thousand years from Adam to Christ and two thousand from Christ until now, then we are entering the seventh day...the final day according to Bible prophecy.

The prophet Joel speaks of this time: "Blow ye the trumpet in Zion, and sound an alarm in my holy mountain: let all the inhabitants of the land tremble: for the day of the LORD cometh, for it is nigh at hand; A day of darkness and of gloominess, a day of clouds and of thick darkness, as the morning spread upon the mountains: a great people and a strong; there hath not been ever the like, neither shall be any more after it, even to the years of many generations" (Joel 2:1,2).

Joel describes a time of terrible trouble and darkness, but at the same time a people of great power such as have never been seen coming forth on earth. These people, I believe, are the ones who go through the process described in the four living creatures to come into the full stature of the Lord Jesus Christ. The Bible tells us that it is through much tribulation that we enter the Kingdom of God...the Kingdom of God being a realm in God not a geographical location. These people are the Overcomers who have been through tribulation and come out in "honor, sanctified, and meet for the master's use, and prepared unto every good work" (2 Tim. 2:21). When I say tribulation, I am not necessarily speaking about a seven year period when the whole world is in great tribulation, but I am referring to the refining fire of God, the crucible that he must put us in, to burn out the dross of our old nature so that Christ can reign totally in us. Then we will be in the kingdom of God regardless of what is taking place in the earth around us. We enter here at different times according to God's workmanship in our lives.

Maturity in Christ requires a deep working of the cross in the life of each individual. The upheaval coming upon us will force us to either die to self allowing Christ to be formed in us or perish. Many believers have not matured in their faith because times have been good. When prosperity reigns and life is good, we seldom seek God. When adversity comes, we start asking questions and seeking deeper meaning in life. This is only human nature (carnality) and it is this carnal nature that has to go if we are to enter into the deep things of God.

The revelation of the four living creatures is for those who are willing to die to self and forsake all to follow Christ. That is the prerequisite for being able to walk in the revelation of

Ezekiel's vision. The coming turbulence will convince many Christians and unbelievers alike that there is nowhere to go to escape the storms except into God's kingdom. The way into this kingdom is not easy. As Jesus said, "...the kingdom of heaven suffereth violence, and the violent take it by force." We will have to force our way into the kingdom. Part of the Greek meaning of these words indicates the idea of "vital activity." We will not enter by doing nothing. We must seek God with our whole heart and obey him in all things. God has much ahead for us if we will work together with him in putting aside the old natural self and embracing our new spiritual life in Christ. The word "force" in the Greek means "to catch up, to snatch away." It is the same word used in the passage about Philip and the Ethiopian Eunuch where the Spirit of the Lord "caught away" Philip and he was immediately at another place! We must seize the kingdom with vital force by seeking God and obeying him in all things, but it is Christ who will catch us up into the spiritual realm where he is.

In past ages when famine, wars or oppression became too great, people could leave their country and find a better land or even a new unexplored land. However, in today's world, these options are no longer available. When terrorists terrorize the world and the threats of chemical, biological or nuclear attacks become reality, where can we go to find safety? When drought, flood, earthquake or famine stalk our land, where can we go when the entire world is under God's judgment? What if the dreaded One World Government becomes a reality and the Antichrist reigns? Where on earth will we go to escape the intrusive eyes of the satellites and the surveillance cameras mounted on every building and street corner?

The only escape will be into God's kingdom but we must be changed before we can enter his kingdom. The four living creatures will reveal that we do not have to leave this earth in order to enter God's kingdom, but that we will be changed (1 Cor. 15:51). We will still be on earth but we will also be in heaven at the same time. This is a great mystery that will unfold before us as we study the four living creatures and unlock their secrets.

The Bible speaks of "the powers of the age to come" (Heb. 6:5). Those who have been willing to forsake all for Christ are even now on the brink of entering into these powers. We are going to have to be so close to God and so one with him that we will be able to walk in his power even as Jesus Christ did. Jesus walked on water, turned water into wine, healed the sick, cast out demons, walked through the midst of an angry mob that tried to kill him, filled a fisherman's net with fish, provided a coin in a fish's mouth, raised the dead and did many more miracles...some recorded in our Bible and some that were never recorded. He is the great I AM. He is what we need him to be when we need him to be it...if, and this is a big "if," we are faithful. If we are not seeking the pleasures of this world and neglecting a relationship with Jesus, if we are not forsaking the cross of Christ, if we are not idolaters, etc. then we can look forward to doing the same miracles Jesus did. In fact, Jesus said, "Verily, verily, I say unto you, He that believeth on me, the works that I do shall he do also; and greater works than these shall he do; because I go unto my Father" (John 14:12).

Do we need to fear being rounded up and sent to a concentration camp as happened in Europe in recent history if we have the ability to just walk out of their midst like Jesus did. Can you imagine that? In the middle of the night, you hear shouts and gunfire, there are trucks and helicopters outside that people are being forced into at gunpoint, and when they break down the door to your house, you just walk away. Or better yet, they just walk past your house as though they never saw it. If the angels are standing guard around your home, the intruders will not dare step foot on your property. God has plans for us to live in this dimension of the supernatural, but we have to go through a process of growth and maturity in him to the point that we are walking in holiness even as Jesus did. This has never been possible before this time, but we are in a new day and God is doing a new thing. We are passing into the age to come. The four living creatures will be showing us how we will transition into this age of miracles.

God is speaking prophetically to many people saying that famine is coming to America. For some people it is already here, but not on the massive scale that is coming. God is speaking about wide-spread famine. We used to have stores of grain and food in this nation, but our government paid farmers not to plant crops. Our grain was given to other nations and now there is no emergency store of food. A few terrorist strikes could shut down our nation's transportation systems. If the trucks don't roll, our grocery stores will not be stocked with food.

Can we store up enough food to live on for a long period of time? Maybe some people can, but many can't afford to or don't have room to store it. Besides, this brings up the questions: Do you keep your food to yourself and let your Christian brother starve? Can you store up enough for yourself, your children and grandchildren...your church...your neighborhood? It can get ridiculous. Jesus might tell us to go to a river or pond and scoop up some fish for dinner (cast your nets down on the right side). He could make a squash plant grow just outside your backdoor or in a pot of dirt on your patio. He could take your small crust of bread and multiply it to feed a multitude. He can and will do all things for his faithful ones in the time of trouble that is even now creeping upon us.

There can be no doubt that these are desperate times for humanity. America, the land of the free and the home of the brave, has turned her back on the biblical principles that this nation was founded upon. The church has become polluted and lost her ability to be salt and light. Yet in the midst of this, God has his remnant, and the plan and purpose of God will be brought to pass on this earth. Let us now begin our detailed examination of Ezekiel One and the four living creatures to learn how we can begin to force our way into the kingdom of God and seize all that Christ has for us in him.

Verse One - Ezekiel...A Type of an End Time Overcomer

Ezekiel 1:1 Now it came to pass in the thirtieth year, in the fourth month, in the fifth day of the month, as I was among the captives by the river of Chebar, that the heavens were opened, and I saw visions of God.

This verse has much to tell us concerning life on earth in the end times when this revelation is to come forth. In this one verse we will be able to uncover information about the stages of development that have been reached by humanity, civilization, the church, and Ezekiel himself. In addition to this, the important location for these visions will be revealed.

The first thing to come to pass, as shown in the number thirty, is that humankind has come to a point of maturity. This is not to say all people are mature but that the working of God has achieved a level of development in us such that some are ready to enter into the things revealed by the four living creatures. The "thirtieth year" speaks of full maturity because of the way we see it used in Scripture. Jesus Christ, King David and Jacob's son, Joseph, after a time of preparation, all began their ministries or reigns at the age of thirty. The priests were also allowed to begin their ministries at age thirty.

When God called Abram forth from Ur of the Chaldees and began the separation and formation of a people to whom he could reveal himself, he started a work that was to continue through several millennia. Down through the ages God has been revealing himself and sifting, separating, and perfecting his people to bring them to maturity in preparation for the coming of his kingdom on earth. Those of us who will be entering into the fullness of God's Spirit will be able to do so because of all the working of God in humanity prior to this time.

Not only are the people of God coming into maturity at this time but also those who have chosen to follow the Devil. There is a fullness of evil coming and indeed already in existence lurking below the surface of our society that is wicked beyond anyone's imagination. The most nefarious Hollywood movie cannot compare to the horror and heinousness that has been laid up by the Devil for this end time showdown between good and evil.

We have no concept of what is just on the horizon. For one thing, we don't truly understand what good and evil really are. We have watched so many thousands of television programs and movies where the good guy was not really good at all according to God's standards, that we are willing to settle for something far less than God is calling us to. We don't truly understand what God's concept of holiness involves. The church in the past has tried to make holiness tantamount to being able to follow a long list of do's and don'ts. If a woman didn't cut her hair, wear makeup or dress in slacks, she was considered holy. God's standard of holiness calls us to be like Jesus. We must spend a lot of time prayerfully pouring over the Scriptures to determine who Jesus was and then to see where we are in comparison. The Holy Spirit will show us and do the work in us as we allow him.

For most of us, the death camps of Nazi Germany would characterize the most diabolical acts ever perpetrated on a civilized society. We've seen pictures of what the Allies found when they entered the concentration camps...human beings that looked like nothing more than skeletons with flesh on them, millions of dead bodies piled up in huge mass graves where bulldozers had shoved them, etc. Surely nothing could be worse than this...or could it? The Holy Spirit witnesses to my spirit that it can and will be even worse than that.

For one thing, the Bible tells us that the Devil and his angels will be cast out of heaven onto the earth. "Woe to the inhabiters of the earth and of the sea! for the devil is come down unto you, having great wrath, because he knoweth that he hath but a short time" (Rev 12:12). Right now the demons are hidden from our sight in the unseen realm called heaven that is all around us. When they are cast out of that realm, we will see them. This is going to be frightening beyond belief. However, if we are God's faithful ones, he has a place of safety prepared for us as indicated in other verses of Revelation 12. Until then, we need to be aware that these evil entities are behind the attacks that come against us. As we use our spiritual weapons we will overcome them. This is all part of the process of coming into maturity. Some call it "new levels, new devils." As we stand in faith against the onslaughts of the enemy, we grow stronger in the Lord. Knowing this helps us face the challenges that inevitably come our way with faith and assurance that God is with us and this is all part of his plan.

In this first chapter of Ezekiel, God will be showing us many more things about his plans for bringing his most mature people into his fullness. After this process is completed, they will be prepared to minister with power and miracles such as the world has never seen. The powerful anointing on these ministries will be for the purpose of bringing the rest of the church to this same level of maturity and completion in Christ. The church will then be seen in her glory and all the nations and peoples of the world will flock to her. Ezekiel 1, the subject of this book, shows us their preparation while Ezekiel 10 reveals their ministry.

Based on the above understandings we may interpret the first phrase of verse one, "Now it came to pass in the thirtieth year," to mean:

Now it has come to pass that humankind has reached a stage of full maturity regarding good and evil and the right moment has arrived for some to come into the perfection of divine order (in the thirtieth year).

In the following phrase, "the fourth month," the number four represents the number of man in his relation to the world as created. (The word "month" is not in the Hebrew text.) It is also the number of material completeness. Based on this understanding of the number four, we can see that as man has come to maturity, so also there has been a coming to completion and fullness of man's creativity. Think of all that man has made out of those things created by God. We have built great cities all over the earth. Through our technology we have been able land a man on the moon, put satellites in orbit around our earth and send probes into outer space with some actually landing on the planet Mars. Our electronic and scientific expertise have produced televisions, cell phones, jet planes, artificial hearts, organ transplants, cloning, surveillance equipment, atomic and hydrogen bombs, chemical and biological weapons, etc. The list is endless. With all our technological advances have come deep ethical issues that some would say have placed men and women in the role of "playing God."

As Eccles. 3:1 tells us, "To every thing there is a season, and a time to every purpose under the heaven." Perhaps God is not going to let us enter any further into this position of "playing God." We may see the time come when we will no longer trust in our technology because it will have reached its zenith and God will say, "That's far enough." After one day of nuclear war, we could find ourselves bombed back into the Stone Age.

Based upon our observations of the number four we may add the following to our first phrase:

Man has come to completeness regarding his relationship to material things and the world (in the fourth) (The word "month" is not in the Hebrew but was added by the translators.)

23

Our next phrase says, "in the fifth day of the month." The Hebrew word for "month," *chodesh*, also means "new moon." According to Andrew Jukes in *Types in Genesis*, "Christ is the sun, the church the moon." We see here that in type, "moon" refers to the church in that the moon reflects the light of the sun with Jesus being our "sun." This is a new moon so we may conclude something new is coming in the church.

In this phrase, the word "fifth" is telling us something about the church (in the fifth of the month [moon = church]). Five is the number of divine strength added to and made perfect in humankind's weakness. It is the number of grace and favor and the number of the fifth kingdom (Daniel) when the kingdoms of this world shall become the kingdom of our Lord and of his Anointed.

According to these explanations we may conclude:

Divine strength is going to be made perfect in humankind's weakness so that the kingdoms of this world can become the kingdom of our Lord and of his Anointed (in the fifth [day]). This is the new thing God is bringing about through his church (of the month).

Ezekiel tells us next that he was "among the captives." We know that historically he was included in the exile from Jerusalem to Babylon in 597 B.C. However, we need to view his captivity from a spiritual perspective for our interpretation of his vision.

In a sense we are all captives either of sin or of righteousness. "Know ye not, that to whom ye yield yourselves servants to obey, his servants ye are to whom ye obey; whether of sin unto death, or of obedience unto righteousness?" (Rom. 6:16). Because God chose Ezekiel for this great vision of the four living creatures, we know he had to have been a slave of righteousness. A slave of righteousness would be a person who no longer lives for himself but lives to please Jesus Christ. In other words, he is a mature Christian who has been willing to take up his cross daily and follow Christ.

Our Christian faith is full of paradoxes...one being that if we are to be truly free, we must be a slave of Jesus. God's ways

24

are always opposite of our ways. In the natural we think that true happiness and freedom would be ours if we could go anywhere we wanted and do anything we pleased. However, this would not bring the joy we would expect because we would by our very nature become enslaved to something...a bad habit, another person, a compulsion, etc. It is an amazing thing that when we give up our right to do as we please and wait upon the Lord's guidance for all we do, we find great joy, peace and freedom.

Ezekiel, then, is a type of a spiritual captive representing a Christian living in the end times who has come to a deep level of maturity in Christ. He is ready to enter into the new things that God will be opening to him that will make it possible for him to transition into a new dimension of spirituality in Christ. We continue our interpretation by saying...

There is a person, representative of mature Christians living in the end times, who has chosen to be a servant of righteousness, a willing slave of the Lord Jesus Christ (among the captives).

Our text tells us he was "by the river of Chebar." "Chebar" means "joining." Our key to knowing to what he was joining is the word "river."

Spiritually speaking this is the river spoken of by Christ when he said, "If any man thirst, let him come unto me and drink. He that believeth on me, as the scripture hath said, out of his belly shall flow rivers of living water" (John 7:37,38). It is Christ who satisfies our thirst and enlightens our minds.

With this in mind, we can see that Ezekiel was positioned close to Jesus, the living water, and because Chebar means "joining," he was joining with him. He represents a person who has more than just right doctrine or knowledge of the Bible. He has a deep and abiding relationship with Jesus Christ. This relationship will be greatly intensified and strengthened as this revelation unfolds.

A closer look at the Hebrew meaning for Chebar will reveal something about how this new depth of relationship is being accomplished. Its more exact meaning is "to join, specifically by means of spells." When we think of spells, we associate them with witchcraft, but there is a deeper insight here. According to

Webster, a spell is a "trance." Both Peter and Paul experienced trances in the New Testament.

Peter explained in Acts 11:5, "I was in the city of Joppa praying: and in a trance I saw a vision, a certain vessel descend, as it had been a great sheet, let down from heaven by four corners; and it came even to me." This vision contained a revelation that the Gentiles were acceptable to God.

In Acts 22:17,18 Paul testified, "And it came to pass, that, when I was come again to Jerusalem, even while I prayed in the temple, I was in a trance; and saw him saying unto me, Make haste, and get thee quickly out of Jerusalem: for they will not receive thy testimony concerning me." The trance further revealed that Paul was to take the Gospel to the Gentiles.

The New Testament Greek word for "trance," ekstasis, reveals it is "a displacement of the mind." Displacement means "to move from its usual place" (Webster).

This person is joining with Christ by moving his mind from its usual place. We all have wrong patterns of thinking and believing that separate us from Christ and keep us from fully entering his kingdom. These patterns of thinking are deeply entrenched in our minds having been laid down over the years by repeated reactions and deductions based on our life experiences. Robert Mulholland states:

> We all have deeply ingrained perceptual frameworks that shape our lives in the world: structures of habit, attitude, perspective, relational dynamics, and response mechanisms. Our perceptual frameworks shape our understanding of God, our understanding of ourselves, and our understanding of others...These frameworks can, and most often do, become our prisons. We find ourselves in bondage to them. Our future becomes a replay of the past. (Mulholland 2000, 33).

These ways of thinking will have to be changed so that Christ can fill our minds with his truth. In order for this to happen, our minds have to be moved from their usual place to a new place of God's truth and the resulting union with Christ. The four living creatures are going to reveal how this is to be accomplished. (It is interesting that both Peter and Paul's trances contained messages about the Gentiles receiving the Gospel so they could be joined to Christ and joined with believing Jews in one faith in Christ!)

Continuing our interpretation of verse one, we can say that...

He is close to Jesus, the living water, and is deepening his relationship with Jesus by means of moving his mind away from its usual place of limited understanding and aligning it with the Word of God (by the river of Chebar).

The last phrase of this first verse states that, "the heavens were opened and I saw visions of God." Heaven means allegorically, "the understanding opened." Since the natural mind is incapable of understanding spiritual realities (Eph. 4:17,18), God must open our understanding as he did for his disciples in Luke 24:45, "Then he opened their understanding, that they might understand the scriptures."

As this person's understanding is opened by God, he begins to see visions. The visions he is seeing are taking place within himself as though he were looking into a mirror and seeing deep within himself. Jesus said, "...behold, the kingdom of God is within you" (Luke 17:21). (Some Bible translators have used the word "among" rather than "within" when translating *entos* in this Luke passage, but according to Strong, it means "within" or "inside.")

If we desire to see Jesus, we must first look within and allow him to transform us into his image before we will see him and his kingdom manifested outwardly. This is because we see according to what is in our own heart. "Unto the pure all things are pure: but unto them that are defiled and unbelieving is nothing pure; but even their mind and conscience is defiled" (Titus 1:15). Our own carnality blocks our view of Jesus. He is within us, closer than the air we breathe, but we are unable to see him because of the veils of our flesh.

In our humanness we believe God thinks, judges and evaluates even as we do, but this is far from the truth. In Psalm 50 where God is calling his people to repentance he says, "...thou thoughtest that I was altogether such an one as thyself: but I will reprove thee..." We must remember that his thoughts and ways are higher than ours and if we are to understand them, we must become like him in character.

The more pure in heart we become, the more good we can see in others and the more accepting we can be of ourselves. God, being perfect in his heart, is able to see us as we will be when his work in us is completed. If we can see ourselves as he sees us, our transformational process will be accelerated because we tend to become like that upon which we focus.

As we continue our study of the four living creatures, God will be revealing the ways he intends to work in us to remove the veils of our flesh that separate us from him. According to our interpretation of this last phrase we can say that...

...his understanding was opened (that the heavens were opened) and he was seeing visions from God within himself (and I saw visions of God).

Now we will combine our understanding of each section into the following spiritual interpretation of verse one:

Now it has come to pass that humankind has reached a stage of full maturity regarding good and evil and the right moment has arrived for some to come into the perfection of divine order (in the thirtieth year). Man has come to completeness regarding his relationship to material things and the world (in the fourth). Now divine strength is going to be made perfect in humankind's weakness so that the kingdoms of this world can become the kingdom of our Lord and of his Anointed (in the fifth). This is the new thing God is bringing about through his church (of the month). There is a person, representative of mature Christians living in the end times, who has chosen to be a servant of righteousness, a willing slave of the Lord Jesus Christ (as I was among the captives). This person is close to Jesus, the living water (by the river), and is deepening his relationship with Jesus by means of moving his mind away from its usual place of limited understanding and aligning it with the Word of God (of Chebar) so that his understanding is being opened (that the heavens were opened) and he is seeing visions from God within himself (and I saw visions of God).

Chapter Two
An Experience with Jesus

Verse Two – God Will Reign in Us
In the fifth day of the month, which was the fifth year of king Jehoiachin's captivity,

This verse begins to reveal more about this new thing God is going to accomplish in his church. Ezekiel, as we learned in verse one, represents a mature Christian living in the end times whose understanding is being opened by God. His mind is being moved from its usual place of limited understanding. He is learning to think differently about some things he has previously thought he understood. Because we have known only "in part," we have formed some solid doctrinal beliefs based on partial knowledge. As that which is perfect comes (Jesus) and opens our understanding, our thinking will need to be adjusted. At this point we will be transitioning from partial knowledge to full revelation necessitating new ways of thinking about some things we thought we fully understood. "...whether there be knowledge, it shall vanish away. For we know in part, and we prophesy in part. But when that which is perfect is come, then that which is in part shall be done away" (1 Cor. 13:8-10).

This concept of knowledge vanishing away may be frightening to some people. I believe the changes coming to the church in these end times will exceed the changes experienced by those who lived in Jesus' day when Old Testament sacrifice was done away by Jesus' perfect sacrifice. Some may find themselves opposing the new thing God is doing because of the fear of falling into error. Others will fear letting go of the comfortable familiarity of the "old" in order to embrace the unknown "new." The only safety will be in having a deep personal relationship with Jesus Christ and his Church and walking in total obedience to the Word of God.

There is a delicate balance to be maintained in being able to receive a new end time revelation without falling into error. I believe I have found the way to be open to revelation and yet keep my feet on solid biblical ground. I do this by being under authority to a godly covering, by having an accountability partner to whom I am very open, by checking all things thoroughly in many places in Scripture, by checking everything in the original languages with concordances and lexicons and by studying large blocks of scripture thereby keeping all things in context. I also check the spirit of what I am learning according to James: "But the wisdom that is from above is first pure, then peaceable, gentle, and easy to be entreated, full of mercy and good fruits, without partiality, and without hypocrisy" (James 3:17). If what God is showing me brings all these qualities into my life and I have thoroughly checked it through all channels available to me, then I can be confident that I am on the right track. And not only that, God himself gives me confirmation through dreams or experiences he brings directly into my life. There is usually no way to have what God is revealing confirmed through someone else's writings because no one else I know of has yet seen some of these things. That is not to say no one else has seen what I see, but I don't know how to connect with them if they have. We can't check the writings of great Christians down through the centuries because they were not allowed to know what God is revealing to us today. However, all things I am learning are consistent with the great biblical truths known down through the church age.

I have noticed over many years in the churches we have served how quickly people will defend a pet doctrine for which they have no real biblical basis. They read someone else's book and will defend what they read until their dying day without ever having studied it, checked the original languages or done research of any kind. This is what will get us into trouble and block our ability to comprehend the new things God desires to do in our lives. We need to know why we believe what we believe. Our conclusions should be based on our own studies and not someone else's. If someone is seeing a revelation about the end times, rather than immediately brand them as heretical because it is different, we need to be as the Bereans of whom the Scriptures say, "These were more noble than those in Thessalonica, in that they received the word with all readiness of mind, and searched the scriptures daily, whether those things were so" (Acts 17:11).

Being able to have our understanding opened by God is predicated on a walk of holiness. In order for God to open our understanding to heavenly things, sin must be removed because we can only see according to what is in our own heart. Revelation is not given to those with the greatest intelligence. Rather revelation comes according to what is in our heart. We see with our heart. The more pure our heart is, the more of God's revelation we are able to comprehend. A heart clouded by sin can be deceived by evil beings in the spiritual realm. Therefore one aspect of heaven being opened involves the cleansing of the sin that indwells us. The closer the manifested presence of Jesus comes to us, the more we recognize our own sinfulness. This leads us to repentance whereby Jesus then burns up the sin and replaces it with his resurrection life. This is a process that takes place incrementally. We will see this process brought to completion as our revelation of the four living creatures unfolds.

At this point it would be good to briefly examine basic biblical truth concerning sin and the nature of man. Chapter One of Ezekiel will be showing us in detail how God will deal with our sin nature as inherited from Adam (referred to as "the old man" in Romans 6) and how the process of sanctification will be brought to completion.

The Bible teaches that our sin nature can be conquered through our identification with the death of the Lord Jesus Christ. We were in him when he died and therefore we also died to sin. This understanding deals with our tendency towards sin as we reckon ourselves dead to sin and alive unto God, but the effects of the sin principle are still at work in our bodies making us susceptible to sickness and the inevitability of aging and death. However, the Bible tells us that, "The last enemy that shall be destroyed is death" (1 Cor. 15:26). God's way of accomplishing this in us, a process that involves our participation, will be revealed further on in our study of Ezekiel One.

Identification with the death of Christ gives us victory over our tendency to choose sin; however, there is another part of us that needs to die daily. This is our self-life that resides in our soul. Jesus taught that, "Whosoever will save his life shall lose it: but whosoever will lose his life for my sake, the same shall save it" (Luke 9:24). The Greek word for "life," *psuche*, actually means "soul." The saving of our soul (sanctification) clearly involves daily decisions concerning whether or not we are willing to obey God and accept his working of the cross in our lives.

When we first asked Jesus into our heart in our initial salvation experience, he came to reside in our spirit. However, our spirit is encapsulated by our soul. If the life of Christ is going to be expressed through our life, our soul that is so absorbed with self-love must be broken. Only in this way will the glorious light of Christ be able to shine forth out of us. Watchman Nee explains it this way:

> Many of God's servants are not able to do even the most elementary works. Ordinarily they should be enabled by the exercise of their spirit to know God's Word, to discern the spiritual condition of another, to send forth God's messages under anointing and to receive God's revelations. Yet due to the distractions of the outward man (*the soul*), their spirit does not seem to function properly. It is basically because their outward man (*the soul*) has never been dealt with. For this reason revival, zeal, pleading and activity are but a waste of time. As we shall see there is just one basic dealing which can enable man to be useful before God: brokenness. (Nee 1965, 9)

This vital principle of life is revealed in John 12 and elsewhere in the Bible. It is a great truth that much of the church has missed. In John when some men wanted to see Jesus, his response to their request was,

> Verily, verily, I say unto you, Except a corn of wheat fall into the ground and die, it abideth alone: but if it die, it bringeth forth much fruit. He that loveth his life shall lose it; and he that hateth his life in this world shall keep it unto life eternal. If any man serve me, let him follow me; and where I am, there shall also my servant be: if any man serve me, him will my Father honour. Now is my soul troubled; and what shall I say? Father, save me

from this hour: but for this cause came I unto this hour (John 12:24-27).

Jesus knew that the only way people would see him (that is, have a revelation of who he was) was for him to die and be resurrected. Then his life would extend into all places and all ages. Jesus is our pattern for life. We don't have to die physically as Jesus did, but we have to die to self in our soul so that the life of Christ can be seen in us. Then we will bear much fruit.

In the natural, if a seed wanted to remain intact in its present condition, it would never yield anything of any use to anyone. If that seed is willing to be put into the cold, hard ground, covered over until it is not visible to anyone, and there become wet and break open, then life will come forth. It will produce fruit along with many seeds that can also become fruit-bearing plants. This is a basic principle of life in the natural and also in the spiritual.

Not only will we become useful for the Master's work, but the degree to which we have been willing to die to self will determine the extent of our capacity to know and enjoy Christ throughout eternity. We all have read promises in the Bible about the wonderful things that are reserved for us in heaven. Some people have described their concept of these rewards as related to a big mansion or a beautiful garment, but Scripture tells us that Christ is our very great reward. "After these things the word of the LORD came unto Abram in a vision, saying, Fear not, Abram: I am thy shield, and thy exceeding great reward" (Gen. 15:1). The Bible tells us that Jesus Christ is the same yesterday, today and forever. He does not change but our capacity to know him does.

God will be able to raise us up into a supernatural dimension of health and safety in him if we are willing to participate by obediently following the mandates of Scripture regarding sin. If our approach to God has been based on our desire to get blessed, we are going to have problems in the days to come. If we have been willing to deny our self and experience the pain of the cross in our lives, we will be progressing into new heights in Christ. Faith, obedience, repentance, love and sacrifice will be vital keys to survival in these end times.

We are told in Rom. 5:10, "For if, when we were enemies, we were reconciled to God by the death of his Son, much more, being reconciled, we shall be saved by his life." Most Christians understand the first half of this verse but have little revelation of the second half. We are successful in our Christian walk when we allow Christ to reign in us and live through us. Each time we take up our cross, deny our self and follow Christ, the result is less of us and more of him. The more he lives in us, the more wisdom and power we have to live, not according to our own desires, but according to his will. When Christ is leading, we will be in the right place at the right time which will be crucial in the coming days of terror and disintegration. This confidence can turn terror into peace for those who walk closely with Jesus and allow him to live his life through them.

The name "Jehoiachin" means "Jehovah has established."

The word "captivity" used here refers to the captivity of all humankind as a consequence of the original sin of Adam and Eve.

Putting together all of the above our spiritual interpretation for verse two is:

The kingdoms of this world are going to become the kingdoms of our Lord (which was the fifth day) and there is something new in the church (of the month); This new thing is that God's grace and favor (which was the fifth year) will reign fully (king) in the lives of those who are living in the captivity that was established by God upon all men at the time of the fall (Jehoiachins's captivity),

Verse Three - Jesus Comes in a Special Way

The word of the LORD came expressly unto Ezekiel the priest, the son of Buzi, in the land of the Chaldeans by the river Chebar; and the hand of the LORD was there upon him.

This verse will give us more information about the life of this person to whom the manifested presence of Jesus is coming. The "word of the Lord" is Jesus, as clearly stated in John 1:14, "And the Word was made flesh, and dwelt among us, (and we beheld his glory, the glory as of the only begotten of the Father,) full of grace and truth."

Jesus is coming "expressly" to this person. "Expressly" means "in a definite way," "specifically," or "particularly." When this experience begins in the believer, there will be no doubt in his/her mind that something powerful and wonderful is happening to him/her because it will be distinct and evident beyond the shadow of a doubt. It will also be individual and specific. This is not something happening to everyone at the same time and in the same way. It is individual, personal and unique. Jesus knows us better than we know ourselves. He knows how to manifest himself to us in a way that will be most meaningful to us as individuals. We will be spiritually ready for this experience at different times because we do not all mature at the same rate.

The name, "Ezekiel," means "God will strengthen." This coming of Jesus is going to strengthen this person. The fact that he is a priest informs us that he is a person who ministers to others, not necessarily as an ordained minister, but as a concerned Christian who helps others. This is an important prerequisite for this new experience with the Lord. Jesus is coming in this way to those who are giving out to others...to those who are willing to sacrifice their own comfort and convenience in order to encourage and minister to others. In this day and age when people fear commitment and have trouble entering into and keeping covenants, God is looking for faithful servants into whom he can pour his life and power.

Our text tells us he is "the son of Buzi." In Hebrew, a son is defined as "a builder of a family name." We know that names are important in Scripture because they represent a person's character. This information tells us that he is a person who has placed importance on the formation of the character of Christ in his life. The word, "Buzi," comes from a root word meaning "contempt," "despised," and "shamed." Therefore we can conclude that this formation of Christ's character has been the result of his godly responses to the contempt, hatred and shame heaped upon him by others.

The Holy Spirit instructs us in Acts 14 saying, "...we must through much tribulation enter into the kingdom of God." The theme of suffering is consistent throughout Scripture. As James teaches, "My brethren, count it all joy when ye fall into divers temptations; knowing this, that the trying of your faith worketh patience. But let patience have her perfect work, that ye may be perfect and entire, wanting nothing."

Only one who has suffered unjustly will be prepared for the coming of Jesus revealed here. We must be willing to enter into the "fellowship of his sufferings" if we are to attain to the resurrection experience revealed in the four living creatures.

In Philippians 3, Paul reveals more about this concept of the fellowship of his sufferings. In the beginning of the chapter he lists all his accomplishments...all the things of the flesh that he trusted in before knowing Christ. Then he says, "But what things were gain to me, those I counted loss for Christ. Yea doubtless, and I count all things but loss for the excellency of the knowledge of Christ Jesus my Lord: for whom I have suffered the loss of all things, and do count them but dung, that I may win Christ." This plainly states that we cannot hold onto all of our earthly riches, all the things that we pride ourselves on be they our accomplishments, our family heritage, our education, etc. If we are to have as much of Christ as possible, we are going to have to give up some things.

Then he continues, "And be found in him, not having mine own righteousness, which is of the law, but that which is through the faith of Christ, the righteousness which is of God by faith: That I may know him, and the power of his resurrection, and the fellowship of his sufferings, being made conformable unto his death if by any means I might attain unto the resurrection of the dead."

After giving up all things in death as we participate in the fellowship of his sufferings, we will be able to experience resurrection life. Once we give up all things as God leads, he may give many of them back to us. Only then, we will not be trusting in them for our righteousness. Also these things will no longer be marred by our carnality but will be coming forth from our spirit. Any of the things God does not return to us, we wouldn't want anyway.

Let me offer an example from my own life. I started taking piano lessons when I was four years old. I got a lot of praise and attention as a little child because of my ability to play the piano. When I was about ten, I started playing the flute. I practiced many hours a day and soon became very proficient. Once again, I received a lot of recognition, awards, scholarships, etc. I did not realize it, but I had formed an identity based on my musical ability. I thought I was a person of value (my own righteousness) based on something I could do well.

As an adult when I became serious about my pursuit of God, he began to deal with me about this false identity. In order to bring it to my attention, God allowed me to be hurt and rejected (a cross experience). It took years for me to understand what God was doing. All the while, I was struggling to use my musical proficiency in the church, but God kept shutting doors in my face (more painful experiences). Over time I was able to understand that I had to die to this by placing it on the altar to God. This was all very painful. It was not just about playing a musical instrument. It was about identity, and identity issues are very painful. Eventually God gave music back to me, but it was no longer my identity. At that point, I no longer had much interest in it. I enjoy good music, but God has given me something so much better...a deeper relationship with him that could only come by knowing that I have value because God loves me and died for me. Out of this revelation our relationship is able to flourish. My righteousness, my significance, is because of what Christ did for me. True depth of relationship with God can only come through our own death and resurrection.

I would like to add another example of the work of the cross in my own life because I believe it helps others understand how this is accomplished. I remember many years ago reading books about the importance of the cross but not understanding how this could be done in my own life. I think examples help us understand this concept much better.

First of all, the cross is not something we initiate. God brings a situation into our life of his choosing that will accomplish our death if we make the right response (which is to not fight against God). This is always an unpleasant circumstance and our natural response is to fight against it. We struggle and do all we know to do to alleviate this circumstance but it just won't go away. As we go through this trial it seems like God is a million miles away and is not answering our cries for help. In situations like this, my husband and I learned to ask the following three questions: (1) Where is God? (2) What is he doing? and (3) How am I responding? Sometimes this helps us sort out the purpose for the situation we find ourselves in. We believe that nothing can come against us in life unless God permitted it. If he allowed it, he has a purpose for it. Sometimes that purpose is so we can experience more of the work of the cross in our life.

A cross experience is not something we cause through direct disobedience and sin like committing adultery or something like that. A cross experience comes into our life as we are doing our best to love and serve God. This circumstance will seem unfair, but then, what they did to Jesus wasn't fair either. This is our opportunity to share in the fellowship of his suffering.

Now to share my experience…it was 1981 and we had just experienced a painful church split leaving us with only a very small congregation meeting in a house. The church split came because we believed and taught the importance of the cross, but we had a board of elders pushing us to preach and teach the prosperity message which we weren't going to do. Some of these elders came to church late every Sunday because they didn't want to miss any of their favorite televangelist's programs. They believed "you can have what you say" and that Christians should never have to endure suffering. Of course, there was no reconciling this situation and we were an independent church with no overseer to help us. These men told us to move on down the pike. They didn't want us in their church any longer.

The only income we had now was from the small group of people who left with us and now met in a house. We never had any idea what our income would be from week to week. We had two children and a mortgage to pay. The only way to make ends meet was for my husband to do whatever work he could find. We lived out in the cornfields of Indiana in a little town of 600 people with not much opportunity for jobs.

Some new people came to our house-church who owned a trucking company. They asked my husband to drive a truck for them on a part-time basis whenever they needed him. It paid minimum wage…not much money but it would help pay the bills. We both had concerns about this job because the trucks were not properly maintained. The rig consisted of a pickup truck with a long trailer attached. There were no brakes on the trailer, so the risks of jack-knifing were high.

One time I went with him on a run to Atlanta, GA. Traffic was horrendous…really scared me. We had a terrible time finding a place to stay because all the motels were full. We finally found something and slept about four hours before heading back to Indiana after the delivery was made. We arrived home late that night literally exhausted. Very early the next morning, the phone rang and the company was telling my husband to immediately make the same run. He had only had four hours sleep. I couldn't go because I had to stay home with our children.

I pleaded with him not to go. I was beside myself with worry. I just knew he was going to die on that run. He would fall asleep, or the truck would jack-knife or he would be killed in all the fast traffic. There was very little money in it anyway. I tried everyway I could think of to get him to listen to me, but he would not. He walked out the door saying he had no choice because we needed the money.

As soon as he walked out the door I heard God speak in my spirit. He said, "Give him to me. He is mine." Then he gave me a scripture. It was Isaiah 43:2, "When thou passest through the waters, I will be with thee; and through the rivers, they shall not overflow thee: when thou walkest through the fire, thou shalt not be burned; neither shall the flame kindle upon thee."

I knew my husband would be safe in God's hands. I also knew that I needed to die to my husband in that I loved him more than I loved God, something I had not recognized. Whenever we love anything more than we love God, that thing is an idol. Also I thought I could protect him better than God could. I got the children ready for school and then spent the rest of the day crying. There was a pain deep inside my heart that I recognized as grief...a grief as strong as the grief I felt when my parents died. I knew I was on the cross and that there would be resurrection life coming after this death.

I love my husband more today than I did then, but I love God even more, and I know God watches over him. Last year, my husband told me he wanted to get a motorcycle. I was shocked. I think riding a motorcycle on the roads and highways today is probably one of the most dangerous things a person could do. My husband said he would not get it if I strongly disagreed, so I prayed. After a few days I knew God was saying, Yes, to the motorcycle. Now I ride on the back of it. That was another hurdle to get over...trusting God for my own protection too.

I hope this helps clarify what the cross is and is not. I had to go through a situation not of my choosing. I did nothing wrong to be in this situation. Actually we were thrust into this situation by our refusal to accept a doctrine that we knew God had not wanted us to embrace. God knew I needed to die to my husband so I could love God even more. The strange thing is, now I love my husband more too...but it is not a possessive, controlling or fearful kind of love. It is true freedom in Christ. This is an example of how the cross sets us free. I didn't have to lose my husband. I only had to go through an experience with him that enabled God to do the work in my heart. Now getting back to our verse in Ezekiel...

All this is taking place "in the land of the Chaldeans." "Chaldeans," means "as demons" or "as robbers." In a world filled with demonic powers and wicked people who are trying to grasp everything for themselves with no concern for the rights of others, God is doing a mighty work in his true church. As the darkness of the One World Government closes in upon us, God is bringing his people into a depth of righteousness that will culminate in their becoming one with him and entering into the realm of his kingdom. An important aspect of this has to do with changing the way we think and aligning our mind with the Word of God "by the river of Chebar."

"The hand of the Lord was there upon him." This Hebrew word for "hand" *yad*, means "the open hand as opposed to *kaph* meaning a closed hand." This open hand indicates power, means and direction. The experience of the four living creatures will take place in a person's life at the direction of Jesus according to his power and his means.

Putting together all of the above information, our interpretation for verse three reads:

Jesus (the word of the Lord) is coming in a definite and individual way (came expressly) to a person whom he is going to strengthen (unto Ezekiel). He is a person who ministers to others (the priest) and whose character has been built (the son) by godly responses to the suffering endured because of the contempt of others who have despised and shamed him (of Buzi). All this is transpiring in a dark and sinful world (in the land of the Chaldeans) where this person is joining with Christ by moving his mind away from its usual place of limited understanding and aligning it with the Word of God (by the river of Chebar). God's power, means and direction to accomplish his divine purpose are upon this person (and the hand of the Lord was there upon him).

Chapter Three
Parables Begin to Form

Verse Four - An Infilling of the Holy Spirit

And I looked, and, behold, a whirlwind came out of the north, a great cloud, and a fire infolding itself, and a brightness was about it, and out of the midst thereof as the colour of amber, out of the midst of the fire.

I believe everyone reading this book is hungry for more of God, and will therefore find this next verse to be very exciting because it depicts the Holy Spirit coming to a believer in the end times. We know this because this verse bears many similarities to Acts 2 where the Holy Spirit fell upon the 120 believers waiting in the Upper Room.

Here we find a "spirit whirlwind" (actual Hebrew definition) that would correspond to the "rushing mighty wind" in Acts. Additionally there is a fire that also reminds us of the Acts passage where tongues of fire appeared above their heads. A new language came to the 120 in the Upper Room, and our next verse here in Ezekiel will show that a new language comes forth here also.

The Holy Spirit came in Acts during the Feast of Pentecost. There were three feasts observed yearly by the Israelites at God's direction. The Feast of Passover which signifies our salvation in Christ, the Feast of Pentecost as a type of the baptism in the Holy Spirit, and the Feast of Tabernacles. The first two feasts have to do with the coming of Jesus to believers. Certainly the last feast must also have to do with Christ's coming. We hear a lot of teaching about the first two feasts and their significance for us today, but very little is said about the Feast of Tabernacles. I believe this Ezekiel verse has much to do with the Feast of Tabernacles regarding the coming of Jesus in the end times.

The Feast of Tabernacles

The Feast of Tabernacles shows us in type what God will be doing for believers in the end times. First of all, this feast came at the time of the harvest. We expect a mighty harvest of souls for Jesus during these end times. During Feast of Tabernacles on the seventh day, the high priest entered beyond the veil into the Holy of Holies into the presence of God...something that happened only once a year. We can expect to enter into God's presence in these end times, and the four living creatures will be revealing to us how this will be accomplished.

At the Feast of Tabernacles (some translations call it "Feast of Booths"), the people left their homes and lived in little booths they made out of the branches of trees. Our body is our house. In these end times, we are going to have a new house, a new body, to dwell in that will never grow old or sick or die. This is what Sue Anne was seeing in her vision of the people who were absolutely perfect in the end times. They had gone through the process depicted in the four living creatures and were in their new bodies.

John 7 will show us more about the things we can expect to experience in the end times as Jesus comes to us in a new way. In this chapter, Jesus goes up to the Feast of Tabernacles going on in Jerusalem at that time. If we view his experience there typically, we will see things that will correspond to what we can expect to experience as Jesus comes to us in this new and special way.

First, Jesus went to the feast secretly. "But when his brethren were gone up, then went he also up unto the feast, not openly, but as it were in secret" (John 7:10). What we will experience in this new infilling of the Holy Spirit will be very personal and something that will not be observed by others. I can say this because I have had this experience. I will share more about this in later chapters.

The next few verses in John reveal the attitudes of the people in Jerusalem at that time towards Jesus. We see the same attitudes in our churches and in the world today. In John the people were talking about Jesus with some saying he was a good man and others claiming that he was a deceiver. Even in churches today there are many that deny the deity of Jesus Christ.

Many at the feast were afraid to speak openly about him because of the Jews. Our ability to speak openly about Jesus is being greatly curtailed as persecution becomes more and more of an issue in America today. I recently saw a news brief about a Christian couple who were fired from their job as caretakers of an apartment building because they had a picture of some flowers on the wall of their office with the depiction under it that said, "Consider the lilies." A new owner took over the building, saw the picture and fired the couple on the spot!

The next verse in John states, "Now about the midst of the feast Jesus went up into the temple, and taught." Beloved, we, as individual believers, are his temple. When Jesus comes to us in this unique experience, he begins to teach us like we have never been taught before! It was shortly after I had this experience of the Holy Spirit coming to me in this very special and personal way, that I began the study the four living creatures that culminated in the writing of this book.

John states regarding his teaching, "And the Jews marveled, saying, How knoweth this man letters, having never learned?" Dear ones, we do not have to have seminary degrees or any special training in order to receive what Jesus wants to show us. For many years I wanted to study the Scriptures but didn't know how. I bought Bible study books with fill-in the blank questions. They were boring. They just did not satisfy my hunger for more of God. After this experience with the Holy Spirit in 1997, the Lord just sovereignly taught me how to study, how to organize my findings so I could always find them (that was a great work of God because I have never been an organized person...my husband will say, Amen, to that!) and then he taught me to write. If you long for more in the Word, the Holy Spirit will teach you...if you give him your life and your time.

The next few verses in John reveal the key to revelation: "Jesus answered them, and said, my doctrine is not mine, but his that sent me. If any man will do his will, he shall know of the doctrine, whether it be of God, or whether I speak of myself." There you have it! If we will do the will of God, if we will say, "Lord, not my will but thy will be done," the Holy Spirit will instruct us and show us "great and mighty things we know not of."

One of the greatest characteristics of those who come into perfection in the end times will be humility. "He that speaketh of himself seeketh his own glory: but he that seeketh his glory that sent him, the same is true, and no unrighteousness is in him" (John 7:18). Jesus was speaking of himself, and it is he who will minister through us in these ends times. God will not entrust his life, power and end time truths into the hands of the prideful. If we have pride in our life, we will use these wonderful things to build a following and get our own way. God will not permit this.

I believe the greatest deterrent to pride is a deep, abiding love relationship with Jesus. When we truly know him and love him, he is all that really matters. The thought of disappointing him or detracting from his glory would be unthinkable. However, there is a powerful enemy (the Devil) that seeks to bring us down at every turn but when the sin nature in us is gone, the enemy will have no way to build a stronghold in our life.

There are so many things we could say about this passage in John. Discernment will be a powerful gift in those who press on into perfection. "Judge not according to the appearance, but judge righteous judgment" (John 7:24). They will be able to see into people's hearts and know them.

And lastly, Jesus spoke of the coming of the Holy Spirit when he was teaching at the Feast of Tabernacles on the last day. He said, "If any man thirst, let him come unto me, and drink. He that believeth on me, as the scripture hath said, out of his belly shall flow rivers of living water. (But this spake he of the Spirit, which they that believe on him should receive: for the Holy Ghost was not yet given; because that Jesus was not yet glorified.)" The Holy Spirit was given at the Feast of Pentecost to those in the Upper Room. The Holy Spirit will be given in much greater magnitude as he comes again at the spiritual Feast of Tabernacles "on the last day." We have much to look forward to!

In Acts, the Holy Spirit was manifested as fire. Fire is also mentioned here, and we know "our God is a consuming fire" (Heb. 12:29). This fire is "infolding" which means "taking up." God is taking him up, but he is not being taken up from the earth. He is entering into a new spiritual dimension in God.

"A great cloud" refers to the presence of God. In Exodus 13 God was in the "pillar of a cloud" that led the Israelites during the day. In 2 Chronicles 5 the presence of God filled the temple like a cloud. He appeared in the cloud upon the mercy seat in the Holy of Holies in Leviticus.

The word "behold," *hinneh*, also means "to see."
"Looked" can also be translated "visions."

Putting together all of the above, our spiritual interpretation of the first half of verse four reads:

In my vision (I looked) I saw (and behold) the Holy Spirit (a whirlwind [rushing mighty wind]) entering into me (came) out of heaven (out of the north). The presence of God (a great cloud), God as a consuming fire (and a fire), was taking me up spiritually into a new dimension in him (infolding).

We saw in the previous verse that Jesus is coming in a personal and definite way to this person. When the Holy Spirit fell on the 120 persons in the Upper Room, it was a distinct experience that did not have to be believed by faith. Everyone knew something new and wonderful had occurred. This coming of Jesus to the individual will also be distinct—the kind of experience where one knows exactly where they were when it happened and that nothing will ever be the same again, but it will be individual and personal.

Even though this experience is definite, it will also be gradual. Our God is so holy and so great that we could not possibly endure His presence should he come in the fullness of his power all at once. Our ability to see and experience him gradually expands as we spend more time in his presence. The more we let go of the things of this world, the more room we will have for him to indwell us. This coming is his indwelling presence, and we visualize it taking place in our mind.

The second half of this verse tells us more about how he was being taken up…

and a brightness was about it, and out of the midst thereof as the colour of amber, out of the midst of the fire.

Our understanding of "brightness" is from Webster's dictionary. Brightness is "the luminous aspect of a color (as distinct from its hue) by which it is regarded as approaching the maximum luminance of pure white or the lack of luminance of pure black."

Jesus is the luminance of pure white. On the Mount of Transfiguration, "his face did shine as the sun, and his raiment was white as the light" (Matt. 17:2). To "regard as approaching" (from Webster's definition of brightness) is to judge by this standard. God judges us according to the standard of perfection seen in Jesus Christ with pure white representing his sinless nature and black representing our darkness of sin.

This brightness (being judged by the standard of Jesus) was "about it," *cabiyb*, which may also be translated "on every side." In other words, this judging is taking place in every aspect of this person's life.

The next word seen in the Hebrew text is *tavek*, translated as "midst." *Tavek* is from an unused root meaning "to sever" or "bisection" and can also be translated "between" or "half." When God judges "between" good or evil in our life according to the standard of the perfection of Jesus, he severs from us the sin (black) and keeps the good (white). You might say that different aspects of our nature are cut in "half."

When this indwelling presence of Jesus comes to the individual, there will be a desire to spend more time alone in his presence and the Bible will begin to open up as never before. As new insights into the Scriptures occur, there will be an exposure of the sin in our own life. The closeness of Jesus will enable us to begin throwing off little distractions and impurities—things of which we have been unaware but that could hinder the depth of relationship we are entering into with our Lord.

During this experience, we will find ourselves entering a stage I call, "others may but you may not." This level of intimacy requires a deeper commitment to holiness than previously understood. The Lord will help us here by giving specific instructions in dreams and visions. As we cast aside these various impurities and distractions, he will sever the desire for these things from our life. As we discard these things, his presence will grow stronger and this will more than compensate for any feeling of loss concerning the things we have released.

As we progress through this period of judging, our ability to see and understand heavenly concepts will be greatly enhanced. It is the fleshly sin in our life that blocks our view of Jesus and his kingdom. This new clarity of vision is seen in the next phrase concerning "colour of amber."

The Hebrew word for "colour," *'ayin*, is sometimes translated "sight."

Amber is, according to Webster, "a yellow or brownish-yellow translucent fossil resin found along some seacoasts." Webster defines "translucent" as "shining through" and "transparent."

Putting these all together, the second half of this verse means:

I was being taken up by means of being judged by God according to the standard of the perfect life of Jesus Christ (and a brightness) in every aspect of my life (was about it). Out of this severing or bisecting of sin from my life (and out of the midst thereof), my sight (as the colour) was becoming translucent and clear (of amber) because of the severing of sin from my life (out of the midst) by the consuming fire of God (of the fire).

The following is our spiritual interpretation of verse four in its entirety:

In my vision (And I looked) I saw (and behold) the Holy Spirit (a whirlwind [rushing mighty wind]) entering into me (came) out of heaven (out of the north). The presence of God (a great cloud), God as a consuming fire (and a fire), was taking me up spiritually into a new dimension in him (infolding). I was being taken up by means of being judged by God according to the standard of the perfect life of Jesus Christ (and a brightness) in every aspect of my life (was about it). Out of this severing or bisecting of sin from my life (and out of the midst thereof), my sight (as the colour) was becoming translucent and clear (of amber) because of the severing of sin from my life (out of the midst) by the consuming fire of God (of the fire).

The following verse will reveal more about the visions of Jesus this person has been experiencing.

Verse Five - Parables...A New Language
Also out of the midst thereof came the likeness of four living creatures. And this was their appearance; they had the likeness of a man.

When the Holy Spirit came upon the 120 persons in the upper room, he initiated a new form of communication, speaking in tongues. It was truly miraculous as they all spoke in other known languages, and people from all over the known world who were visiting in Jerusalem heard their own language being spoken by people they acknowledged could not possibly have known their language. Great power came upon the church and many unbelievers came to a saving knowledge of the Lord Jesus Christ. This was at the time of the Feast of Pentecost.

Since that time many believers have had the experience of speaking in other tongues. These are seldom known earthly languages but are rather unknown heavenly languages. There are many believers who don't think speaking in tongues still happens today, but I know it does because I have had the experience. I speak in other tongues everyday as I pray and minister. I don't know what I am saying but God does and so do the demons. Many times I have cast out demons and used speaking in tongues as a forceful weapon against them. They have spoken out of the person in whom they were manifesting saying things like, "Don't talk to me like that. You have no right to say that to me. Oh, no, don't say that." Then they leave...so clearly something is being said that is spiritual in nature.

I had a friend, who has gone to be with the Lord, who had the experience of actually speaking in another known language when she was at the altar in a church with a group of people praying. She was praying in her prayer language when a man near her got very excited about what she was saying. She had spoken a message to him about a loved one in another nation that he happened to be praying for at that exact time. She had no idea that she had said anything in a known language. She was just praying to God and the Holy Spirit spoke through her mouth in another language to the man standing next to her.

When I received the gift of speaking in tongues, I had been praying for the baptism of the Holy Spirit and believed that speaking in tongues would be the proof that I had received that gift. However, it did not happen at all as I expected. I kept waiting for God to take over my mouth and make me speak, but others around me at the time encouraged me to open my mouth and believe by faith that the words would be there. When I did as they said by faith (feeling a little embarrassed by what might or might not happen) to my surprise the words came pouring out. I thought I would see the words in my mind and then speak them. That is not the way it was, however. I found that as I spoke the language, it came up from my spirit in the area of my heart and completely bypassed my mind! It flowed very fast. I could do it any time I chose or I could choose not to do it at all. It was all at my volition.

I want to state here that speaking in tongues was not nearly so life changing as the way the Word of God opened up to me immediately after that experience. The very next day as I read the Bible, I could really understand what I was reading for the first time. All of a sudden the Bible became very interesting and I could hardly put it down. Before this I would read out of duty, but now I read from desire and I knew God was speaking to me through his Word. That was a supernatural experience.

Two months later God sent us to pastor a different church. Our second Sunday there, he brought into our church a man with an incredible gift of prophecy who began to daily prophesy to us about the call God had placed on our lives to minister in the end times. This prophet, Wayne, had a strange sounding prayer language. It consisted of one word..."beebity." When he prayed in tongues it was "beebity, beebity, beebity!" Wayne said he had prayed and asked God for more of a language but God said no. However, when Wayne prophesied he started out praying in his prayer language, and then all of a sudden it would change and sound like Chinese or some other known language. Then he would prophecy. You always knew when Wayne was going to give you a word because his language would change. Rather than prophecy, I think his gift would more accurately be called the gift of tongues and interpretation (1 Cor. 12:10). Whatever it was, it was incredibly accurate and supernatural. You knew God was speaking to you telling you what was in your heart and giving you a word that was encouraging and instructive.

That was back in 1972. I still have those prophecies I recorded and typed up. Over the years, some very difficult years, I would get those out and read them over and over again. There have been other prophets along the way that have given us encouraging words. Without these wonderful gifts of the Holy Spirit, I don't know how we could have overcome through the difficult circumstances we have encountered during our 35 years in pastoral ministry.

I say all this by way of preparation for what I am about to say concerning a new language God is presenting to us in these end times. This new language will be revealed as we unlock the secrets of the four living creatures. Similar to my experience of speaking in other tongues, this new language will be something we participate in by faith. It will be exercised at our volition. It will be life changing. It will bring us into God's presence where we will find encouragement and strength. By contrast to speaking in other tongues, this communication will be silent and will be seen as visions in our mind. Speaking in tongues is an outward manifestation. The visions of allegorical stories are an inward reality that leads us toward perfection and into heaven.

Let's look at this verse now in depth:

Also out of the midst thereof came the likeness of four living creatures. And this was their appearance; they had the likeness of a man

Likeness

A very important word in this verse is "likeness." "Likeness," *demuwth*, in the Hebrew, means "similitude." A similitude is "a parable or allegory." We all know that parables are stories and that Jesus used parables when he taught the multitudes. These stories conveyed important messages to the people. A parable, *mâshâl*, is defined as a simile; therefore, we can say that "likeness" is a parable and it is also a simile. As we examine this further, we will see that the new language of the Spirit will be inward, in the form of pictures and stories (parables) that enable us to communicate with God in a deeper way.

A simile is a figure of speech in which one thing is likened to another or a comparison using "like" and "as." Jesus used simile when he said, "The kingdom of heaven is like a grain of mustard seed," and "The kingdom of heaven is like leaven," and "The kingdom of heaven is like a treasure hid in a field." Jesus used similes or parables exclusively when he taught the multitudes. "All these things spake Jesus unto the multitude in parables; and without a parable spake he not unto them" (Matt. 13:34).

The concordance also states that a parable is "superiority of mental action." Our Bible, the greatest book ever written, is full of parables or similes. We know Jesus used them but we need to see that the Old Testament is also replete with simile—Song of Solomon for example, "My beloved is like a row or a young hart. As a lily among thorns, so is my love among the daughters."

The Holy Spirit teaches us in Isa. 55:8,9 that, "...my thoughts are not your thoughts, neither are your ways my ways, saith the LORD. For as the heavens are higher than the earth, so are my ways higher than your ways, and my thoughts than your thoughts." God chose to reveal many of these thoughts and ways to us via parables. Since a parable is "a superiority of mental action," and we are to move our mind away from its usual place (Chebar), what better way to do it than to begin thinking in parables?

The Hebrew word for "parable," *mâshâl*, is from the root word, *mâshal*, which means "to rule," "to make have dominion," "have power" and "governor." As we use this superiority of mental action (parables) to move our mind from its usual place (Chebar), we will begin to rule or take dominion over the aspects of our being that have been beyond our control—our emotions and our physical body. Parables will give us the power to govern our entire being and bring it into subjection to our spirit that is united with Christ in purpose. This will bring our entire being into the kingdom of God—the place where Jesus rules over all.

In Matthew after it states that Jesus spoke to the multitudes only in parables, it says that he did so to fulfill what was spoken by the prophet when he said, "I will open my mouth in parables; I will utter things which have been kept secret from the foundation of the world." It is clear from this passage that the secrets of the end times that have been kept secret from the foundation of the world will be revealed through parables or similes. Over and over again when Jesus spoke of the kingdom of God, he used parables. The revelation brought forth through the four living creatures will show us that we must literally use parables or think parabolically in order to enter fully into the kingdom.

Continuing on with verse five, our next word is "four." As we previously learned, "four" is the number of the earth or man in his relationship to earth.

"Living creatures," as we shall see, are people. Jesus said in Mark 16, "Go ye into all the world, and preach the gospel to every creature. He that believeth and is baptized shall be saved; but he that believeth not shall be damned." We preach the Gospel to human beings because we are the only species capable of comprehending it.

Paul teaches in 2 Corinthians 5, "Therefore if any man be in Christ, he is a new creature: old things are passed away; behold, all things are become new." These living creatures in Ezekiel 1 are those who are in Christ and have put off the old and put on the new. They are the ones ready to go forward with Christ into new realms of the kingdom. Ezekiel is one of these living creatures. Jesus Christ himself is referred to as "the image of the invisible God, the firstborn of every creature" (Col. 1:15).

The next important word we need to examine in verse five is "appearance." This word in Hebrew, *mar'eh,* may also be translated "visions."

In parables, abstract concepts of truth are conveyed in word pictures that can be seen in the imagination. For example, Jesus could have said, "Not all people will respond to the Gospel in the same way" (an abstract concept), but instead he said, "Behold, a sower went forth to sow, and when he sowed, some seeds fell by the way side..." Immediately a picture comes to our mind. If we focus on that picture with our imagination, it takes on the form of a vision.

The word, "man," refers to the one man, Jesus Christ. "For if through the offence of one many be dead, much more the grace of God, and the gift by grace, which is by one man, Jesus Christ, hath abounded unto many" (Rom. 5:15). If living creatures refer to human beings then "man" has to refer to a particular man—someone above the status of a creature. This is Jesus Christ who has been glorified and bears the name that is above all names.

Keeping in mind all of the above, we may interpret verse five as saying:

As this severing of sin from my life was transpiring (also out of the midst thereof), parables began to come forth (came the likeness) about mature Christians living on the earth (of four living creatures). These parables were in the form of visions (and this was their appearance). These parables were also (they had the likeness) about the Lord Jesus Christ (of a man).

Our spiritual interpretation is referring to the living creatures as being plural. They are plural in the sense that many Christians in the end times will have this experience as they are transformed into the image of Christ. However, there is a sense in which the living creatures need to be viewed as singular. As this person, represented by Ezekiel, begins to see visions of parables, the parables will be about himself and Jesus Christ, not other people. This will be a very private experience between the individual and God, an experience that will result in this person's total transformation.

When the Holy Spirit came to the 120 persons in the upper room, they received new languages as they began speaking in other tongues. With the outpouring of the Holy Spirit in this Ezekiel passage, a new language is introduced here too. This is the language of parables in the form of visions. This will be the language required to bring our understanding of the kingdom of God to new dimensions, touching our heart and our physical body.

The living creatures represent a person who has put off the old and embraced the new—a mature Christian who is ready to enter fully into the kingdom of God in the last days. He has won many victories by pulling down strongholds and taking every thought captive to Christ, but there are still aspects of his being that have not yet yielded totally to the Lord.

We all have things lodged deeply in our hearts of which we are unaware. Or if we are aware of them, we can't seem to change them. No matter how much we pray, obey and live the Word, some parts of us never seem to change. It is like they have a life of their own. The story visions we will be learning about will be able to reach these parts of our being. They will also be able to begin to bring the physical body under the Lordship of Jesus Christ. This new language of parables, or stories, seen as visions in our mind will begin to cause all parts of our being to become aligned with the Word of God.

Jesus taught that parables reveal the mysteries of the kingdom of God and that if we understand with our heart, we will be healed.

> And the disciples came, and said unto him, Why speakest thou unto them in parables? He answered and said unto them, Because it is given unto you to know the mysteries of the kingdom of heaven, but to them it is not given. For whosoever hath, to him shall be given, and he shall have more abundance: but whosoever hath not, from him shall be taken away even that he hath. Therefore speak I to them in parables: because they seeing see not; and hearing they hear not, neither do they understand. And in them is fulfilled the prophecy of Esaias, which saith, By hearing ye shall hear, and shall not understand; and seeing ye shall see, and shall not perceive: For this people's heart is waxed gross, and their ears are dull of hearing, and their eyes they have closed; lest at any time they should see with their eyes and hear with their ears, and should understand with their heart, and should be converted, and I should heal them (Matt. 13:10-15).

The mysteries of the kingdom of God must be understood with the heart. In order to understand with the heart, we must make sure that the ears and eyes of our heart are neither dull nor closed. People who have gone to church, heard the Word of God and chosen not to obey it have hardened their hearts so that they are not able to see or hear the things of the kingdom. Those who hear, understand and obey the Word have good hearts and are able to move into the revelation of Ezekiel's vision.

This is a perfect example of the wise and foolish virgins of Matthew 25. If one has hardened one's heart through disobedience through the years, there will be no oil in one's lamp. It will be impossible to suddenly have a heart ready to enter into this new language of parables. Those who have obeyed the teaching of 2 Cor. 10:5 by "casting down imaginations, and every high thing that exalts itself against the knowledge of God, and bringing into captivity every thought to the obedience of Christ" will have a disciplined mind capable of focusing on the parables. Parables in the form of visions will not only bring healing to the physical body but also will deepen our relationship with Jesus and open our understanding to heavenly realities.

The Importance of Story

Parables are stories that emphasize a certain truth that the teller wants his audience to understand. Parables and allegories are similar in that both forms of writing use metaphor in order to get abstract ideas across through storytelling. Many aspects of our faith are abstract. If we can personify these concepts by seeing them in the form of a story vision in our mind, they become more real and have more power to change us.

Each person's life is a story. If Jesus had not come to earth in human form and lived with men who could write his story, it would be very difficult for us to conceive of God. As we read the Bible, we can form pictures of his life in our mind. We know his story.

Parables seen as visions in our mind enable us to put the story of our life together with the story of Christ's life in a relational way that brings the presence of God into the very depths of our being. In this book, you will read several of my stories that have brought healing to my own soul and body. Some of these are quite long and detailed. They do not perfectly fit the definition of a parable in that parables are short stories. They could more properly be termed allegories that contain within them parables because they are longer and contain several messages and parables convey usually only one truth. However, I have chosen to call them all parables because switching back and forth from the terms parable to allegory could be confusing.

Most of my healing parables have not been as long as some of them written here. I found as I wrote they just started expanding as I described Jesus, the scenery, my feelings, our conversation, etc. Hopefully my stories will help others gather ideas that will help them form their own parables. Parables can be based on specific scriptures, or they can just be scriptural in nature. The Holy Spirit will help us when we sincerely seek to draw closer to him in this way.

Chapter Four
The Way to Divine Health Begins

Verse Six – Parables Begin in a Natural Heart and Mind
And every one had four faces, and every one had four wings.

The Natural Heart

The next major word to decipher for our spiritual interpretation is "faces." The concordance defines the face as "the part that turns" and also "sight." In the physical realm, if we want to look at something, we turn our face towards it. In the spiritual realm, we turn our heart towards that thing we desire to see and understand spiritually. Our heart determines the course of our life as it turns us in different directions. When someone looks at our face, they see our countenance, but our countenance is determined by what is in our heart.

The concordance defines the heart, *leb*, as the "feelings, the will, the intellect or the center of anything." Obviously the heart is an extremely important part of our being and would be included in any detailed revelation of God's dealing with humankind. The Bible has much to say about the human heart and we will learn more in our study as we see the "faces" of the four living creatures are actually the "heart."

Discovering an Important Part of Our Mind

Wings

The wings of a bird enable it to fly—to soar high above the earth where it can see from an elevated position and escape dangers that would otherwise destroy it. Human beings also have wings—the wings of the imagination. Our imagination can transport us in our mind any place we want to be. It is a gift from God that enables us to transcend the mundane and soar into new heavenly dimensions with Christ. As Glenn Clark explains in his book, *The Soul's Sincere Desire*:

The imagination is of all qualities in man the most godlike—that which associates him most closely with God. The first mention of man in the Bible is where he is spoken of as an 'image' (Gen. 1:26): 'Let us make man in our image, according to our likeness.' (Clark 2001)

God could have said only "Let us make man in our image." How interesting that he added "according to our likeness." Now that we know the word for "likeness" also means "parables" a new understanding emerges. We come into his image (in the sense of being perfected) according to the parables that we see in the visions of our imagination. Glenn Clark continues by saying,

The only place where an image can be conceived is in the imagination. Thus man, the highest creation of God, was a creation of God's imagination. The source and center of all man's creative power—the power that lifts him above the level of brute creation and gives him dominion over all the fish of the sea, the birds of the air, and the animals that move and creep on the earth—is his power of making images, or the power of the imagination. The imagination of man is but the window or door which, when thrown open, lets the divine life stream into our lives. (Clark 2001)

Some Christians have been taught it is wrong to use the imagination—that people's imaginations are only evil. Actually there is no place in the Scriptures to support that belief. Scripture does say several places that the imagination of persons was evil, but that is because they were evil people. A righteous person will see good things in his/her imagination.

If the imagination is evil and not to be used, then King David sinned when he prayed his last recorded prayer at the offering of gifts for the temple to be built by his son, Solomon. David prayed that people would use their imaginations when he prayed, "O LORD God of Abraham, Isaac, and of Israel, our fathers, keep this for ever in the imagination of the thoughts of the heart of thy people, and prepare their heart unto thee" (1 Chron. 29:18).

David is a type of the church today—the church that has restored praise but been at war. There have been many wars between churches and within churches as members bicker and fight over various issues. These wars are an outcropping of the battles that rage internally within each person. As the church transitions into maturity, the wars will cease and Solomon (meaning peace, perfect) will reign. The first place peace must reign is within each individual. It is the "imagination of the thoughts of the heart" of God's people that will "prepare" (and perfect in the original Hebrew) the hearts of his people unto him.

Scripture tells us Solomon came forth from the loins of his father, David. Solomon said, "And the LORD said unto David my father, Whereas it was in thine heart to build an house unto my name, thou didst well that it was in thine heart. Nevertheless thou shalt not build the house; but thy son that shall come forth out of thy loins, he shall build the house unto my name" (1 Kings 8:18,19).

The New Testament Greek word for "loins" is in 1 Pet. 1:13 where we read, "...gird up the loins of your mind." The word "loins," *osphus*, means "procreative power." The word "mind" is *dianoia*, which can also be translated "imagination." The procreative power of the mind is the imagination. Every great invention was first seen in someone's imagination. Beethoven, being deaf, heard his great Ninth Symphony in his imagination before he wrote it. Every creative work of man was first conceived in the imagination.

Solomon, the church at rest, filled with the wisdom and riches that will astound the world, will come forth from the loins (parables formed in the imagination) of the present church, David. The church will be built stone by stone of individual lives of those who have "kept this forever in the imagination of the thoughts of their heart" that they might "prepare (perfect) their heart" unto God.

If I am to come into perfection in God, then I have to begin to see myself that way. The only way I can do this is to use my imagination to begin to see myself as God sees me. He sees me as already complete in Christ. It is easy for me to look in a mirror and see all manner of imperfections in my appearance. It is easy to compare myself with someone else and feel that I fall short of what I should be. The Bible tells us we are not to compare ourselves with others. I am to look into the mirror of the Word, see what I am supposed to be there, and begin to see myself in that light. As I focus upon what I can become in God, I will begin to become that upon which I have set my focus.

In addition to seeing myself complete in Christ, I need to focus on Christ's presence with me at all times. His Word says that he is always with me but if I am to live as though that is true, I need to imagine him with me everywhere I go. I can only do this by using my imagination. When I take a brisk walk around my neighborhood every day, I imagine him walking with me and I talk to him as we go along. I know this pleases him and I am much closer to him because of doing this.

I used to walk without imagining him with me. It was boring and there were many days when I didn't walk because it was such a dreaded chore. Then when I heard the Lord say I was to imagine him walking with me, it took on a whole new dimension. Now I actually look forward to the walks. I feel so invigorated by them. I praise the Lord, talk over scriptures with him and ask him questions as we walk. When I return home, I often find he has opened the scripture to me in a new way or answered my questions.

The church has been afraid of the imagination when actually it is a gift from God from which all creativity flows. My family and our whole church used to attend annual week-long Bible seminars in the late 1970s and early 80s that were taught all over the nation. We attended the one in Indianapolis, IN and there were literally thousands in attendance. This teacher always devoted one evening to the concept of meditation. He said we should memorize large portions of Scripture and then meditate on these passages. I distinctly remember him saying we could meditate by drawing a picture of something. He said, by way of example, that we could draw a picture of righteousness.

I wanted more than anything to do what this man said. I memorized whole chapters of Scripture, but never could figure out how to meditate. I tried to draw a picture of righteousness, but just could not think of how to do it. What I resorted to doing was diagramming sentences (as I learned to do in English class) of the passages I was memorizing! That was the only way I could think of to picture something. I realize something now. That teacher never mentioned the imagination. He knew that if he did, many people would stop attending the seminars. If he had said to imagine righteousness taking place in a life situation, I would have understood and been able to do it. It was many, many years later that the Holy Spirit taught me how to meditate by teaching me to use my imagination.

It was Solomon who wrote the book of Proverbs (or we could say Parables). The Hebrew word for proverbs, mâshâl, is the same word translated "parables," so in the Old Testament, proverbs and parables are the same. A parable involves making an abstract concept into a picture story that can be seen in the imagination. Those of us who become part of the "Solomon" church will minister in great wisdom and power via parables as we teach others about perfecting their heart unto God. Let's look at just a few of the many passages from Proverbs that use allegory to help us see a picture of an abstract concept:

- Instructions from parents are a graceful ornament on the head and chains on the neck.
- Evil deeds are a net for our feet.
- Understanding is silver and hidden treasure.
- The Lord is a shield to the upright.
- Wickedness is a crooked path.
- Wisdom is length of days in the right hand and riches and honor in the left.
- Wisdom is the tree of life.
- An industrious worker is like an ant.
- Faithfulness in marriage is like drinking water from your own cistern.
- The words of your mouth are a snare.
- Poverty comes like a prowler.
- Immorality is fire in the bosom that burns the clothes.
- Adultery is like walking on hot coals that burn the feet.
- Wisdom calls us to eat at the great banquet she prepares.
- Immorality is stolen water and bread eaten in secret.
- The mouth of the righteous is a well of life.

- A rich man's wealth is his strong city.
- A lazy man is like vinegar to the teeth and smoke to the eyes.
- A lovely woman who lacks discretion is as a ring of gold in a pig's snout.
- An excellent wife is a crown of her husband.

These are just a few of the allegorical concepts revealed to us through Proverbs. Each one suggests a picture to our imagination that makes it more powerful than mere words. If a person considering immorality pictures it as a fire in their bosom that burns their clothes and like walking on hot coals that burn their feet, then it can help them choose righteousness more so than just words of warning.

Hidden beneath the surface of the Word in the original languages, one may find many places where the use of the imagination is encouraged. Paul prayed in Eph. 1:18 for the "eyes" of their "understanding" to be "enlightened." If we examine this word for "understanding" in the original Greek we find it is the same word found in the 1 Peter passage above, *dianoia*, meaning "imagination." So Paul is praying for the eyes of their imagination to be enlightened (*photizo* meaning "made to see.") Why? So that they might know, as the passage continues, "what is the hope of his calling, and what the riches of the glory of his inheritance in the saints, and what is the exceeding greatness of his power to us-ward who believe, according to the working of his mighty power, which he wrought in Christ, when he raised him from the dead, and set him at his own right hand in the heavenly places..." These things concerning our inheritance and great power are things meant for the end times church—realities we will enter into as we use our imagination to see the parables the Holy Spirit will be inspiring us to see.

This Greek word, *dianoia*, meaning "imagination" is also found in 1 John 5:20, "And we know that the Son of God is come, and hath given us an understanding (*dianoia*), that we may know him that is true, and we are in him that is true..." We can say then that the Son of God has come to give us an "imagination" that we may know him and know that we are in him. When we use our imagination to envision Jesus, we come to know him in a way that would not be possible with mere words and abstract concepts. We need to visualize ourselves as being in Christ and he in us in order to appropriate the glorious promises of what it means to be "in Christ" and to have "Christ in us."

Jesus said, "And thou shalt love the Lord thy God with all thy heart, and with all thy soul, and with all thy mind (*dianoia*—imagination). We are to use our imagination when we love Jesus. We can say the words "I love you" to Jesus and perhaps not feel the emotion that should be connected with the words. However, worship comes into a whole new dimension when we use our imagination to envision the man Jesus and say those same words while looking into his eyes of love and compassion.

These are all examples from the New Testament, but the Old Testament also encourages us to use our imagination. A powerful verse for peace in the midst of chaos is found in Isa. 26:3, "Thou wilt keep him in perfect peace, whose mind is stayed on thee..." The Hebrew word for "mind" here is yetser, which also means "imagination." God will keep us in perfect peace when our imagination is sustained upon him. This takes practice. If we train our imagination to picture Jesus daily as we worship and pray, then when chaos and terror reign in our land, we can go to this place of safety in our mind. It is more than just imagination. Our imagination within our heart is our gateway into the very presence and power of God.

Another Old Testament word for "imagination" is *hagah*, but it is usually translated as "meditate." The following passages where "meditate" occurs can also refer to the imagination:

Psa. 1:2 But his delight is in the law of the LORD; and in his law doth he meditate day and night. (Begin to imagine yourself as being righteous in every circumstance in your life as you envision Jesus with you wherever you go.)

Psa. 63:5,6 My soul shall be satisfied as with marrow and fatness; and my mouth shall praise thee with joyful lips when I remember thee upon my bed, and meditate on thee in the night watches. (When you go to bed at night, in your imagination see yourself in a lovely place with Jesus and tell him about your day.)

Psa. 77:12 I will meditate also of all thy work, and talk of thy doings. (Imagine yourself talking with Jesus about all the great things he has done and is doing in your life.)

Psa. 143:5 I remember the days of old; I meditate on all thy works; I muse on the work of thy hands. (Imagine yourself looking at a lovely sunset with Jesus and talking to him about how much you enjoy the beauty of his works all around you.)

Josh. 1:8 This book of the law shall not depart out of thy mouth; but thou shalt meditate therein day and night, that thou mayest observe to do according to all that is written therein: for then thou shalt make thy way prosperous, and then thou shalt have good success. (If you are having a problem being righteous in any area of your life, picture yourself and Jesus with you as you make godly decisions about every circumstance you are facing.)

As we can see from these examples, the Bible in the original languages of Hebrew and Greek says much more about the imagination than is seen on the surface.

The Pilgrim's Progress, often acclaimed as the greatest Christian work written in the English language, was the result of one man's imagination used to write what he called a "fable" to illustrate Christian truth. The complete title was, *The Pilgrim's Progress from this world to that which is to come*. This title describes what I have seen here in the four living creatures...by using our holy imagination in conjunction with the Holy Spirit, we are enabled to progress from the limitations of this world into the supernatural powers of the age to come which is the kingdom of God. We do this as we make parables seen as visions in our mind that incorporate God's truth, thereby enabling our spirit to rule over our soul and body resulting in new levels of holiness and healing.

Oswald Chambers wrote of the importance of using our imagination with his comments regarding Isaiah 26:3, "Thou wilt keep him in perfect peace, whose mind (imagination) is stayed on thee:"

> Is your imagination stayed on God or is it starved? The starvation of the imagination is one of the most fruitful sources of exhaustion and sapping in a worker's life. If you have never used your imagination to put yourself before God, begin to do it now. It is no use waiting for God to come; you must put your imagination away from the face of idols and look unto Him and be saved. Imagination is the greatest gift God has given us and it ought to be devoted entirely to Him. If you have been bringing every thought into captivity to the obedience of Christ, it will be one of the greatest assets to faith when the time of trial comes because your faith and the Spirit of God will work together. (Chambers February 11)

In another entry, Chambers again speaks of the imagination as related to a passage in Isaiah 40:26, "Lift up your eyes on high, and behold who hath created these things:"

> The people of God in Isaiah's day had starved their imagination by looking on the face of idols, and Isaiah made them look up at the heavens, that is, he made them begin to use their imagination aright...
> The test of spiritual concentration is bringing the imagination into captivity. Is your imagination looking on the face of an idol? Is the idol yourself: Your work?...If your imagination is starved, do not look back to your own experience; it is God Whom you need. Go right out of yourself, away from the face of your idols, away from everything that has been starving your imagination. Rouse yourself, take the gift that Isaiah gave the people, and deliberately turn your imagination to God.
> One of the reasons of stultification in prayer is that there is no imagination, no power of putting ourselves deliberately before God...Imagination is the power God

gives a saint to posit himself out of himself into relationships he never was in. (Chambers February 10)

Leanne Payne points out that the use of the imagination and symbol are necessary for getting truth from our head down into our heart. To not use the imagination is to...

> leave people vulnerable to non-Christian groups that have empathy for the unhealed psyche. Those heavily into Jungian spirituality, the New Age, or some other form of Neo-Gnosticism and paganism know the language of the heart. They recognize that this language is metaphoric and symbolic. They are not afraid to visualize. (Payne 1985, 180)

There is one more scripture I want to add here, "...we look not at the things which are seen, but at the things which are not seen: for the things which are seen are temporal; but the things which are not seen are eternal" (2 Cor. 4:18). The only way we can look at things that are not seen is to use our imagination.

Hopefully these many illustrations of the importance of the imagination will help release those who have been fearful of using their imagination. Truly it is a vital part of our mind and a wonderful gift from God. Now that we have established that "wings" are the imagination, let us continue our examination of verse six.

Parables Begin in the Natural Imagination

And every one had four faces, and every one had four wings.

The word "four" appears twice here. Remember "four" is the number of creation and man in his relation to all that is created or the earth. The subject here is still parables as in the previous verse.

Keeping these things in mind, here is our interpretation of verse six:

These parables (every one) came from hearts (faces) that related to things of the earth (four). These parables also (every one) came from imaginations (wings) that related to things of the earth (four).

Or for easier reading we could say,

These parables came from hearts and imaginations that related to the earth—saw and understood earthly things.

We can only understand and envision things according to what we know of the earth. For example, I can only imagine colors I have seen on earth. People who have had glimpses into heaven tell me there are colors there that we don't have on earth. I can't imagine that. This verse is telling us that the parables, as they are beginning to be formed, are about earthly things because this is all the person has ever known.

When God revealed to me in a personal way his desire to heal me of hay fever, he told me to begin imagining being with him in some beautiful place—anyplace in his creation that appealed to me where hay fever would be a problem. He wanted me to experience a new depth of closeness with him that would come from envisioning him. Out of this new dimension of being with him, I would learn to bring the truth of his Word out of the abstract and into the reality of my daily life. This would result in my being healed of hay fever.

I began to work on forming a scene in my imagination based on a lovely place I remembered from childhood. It was a beautiful meadow I had seen on the side of a mountain in Colorado many years ago. I placed all the wildflowers I could think of into the meadow and made it as beautiful as possible.

Then I brought Jesus into the picture. We walked through the meadow filled with flowers and surrounded by tall trees. As we sat down in an area of lush green grass, Jesus began speaking to me of his desire to heal me. (Out of my heart, I made up our conversation based upon what I knew about Jesus and thought he would say.) He said to me that he had made the lovely things around us (all of which I was allergic to) with the intent of blessing me. It was not his will for the pollen from the trees, grasses and lovely flowers to make me sick. He wanted me to come often to this meadow in my imagination and visualize myself enjoying the beauty of his creation with no sickness. He would meet me there and we would talk about the healing scriptures.

I learned to go to the meadow in my mind whenever my nose ran uncontrollably and remain at the meadow until the allergy attack subsided. I memorized many healing scriptures to talk about with Jesus while I was there. I had to return there several times a day, but I made it through the summer without the aid of allergy shots or antihistamines, (although I could have used these if I so chose, but they weren't effective anyway). I was definitely better but not yet fully healed. That was thirteen years ago. Each summer the allergy problem has become less and less of an issue in my life. I have actually had a summer or two with no allergy symptoms at all. During that thirteen year period, as allergies continually decreased their hold on my life, I learned that whenever I had a drippy nose, it was a signal from the Lord that he wanted me to stop whatever I was doing and spend time in his presence. That would always take care of the problem.

Our study of the four living creatures will reveal that God intends for his people to walk in divine health in the end times. Healing will come gradually as we come closer to God by dying to the things of the world and walking in holiness.

A walk of holiness is not achieved by living according to a set of rules. Holiness is purity of heart. It is a heart free from idolatry that is willing to say, not my will but thy will be done in all things. When we love Jesus more than anything else on earth...more than husband, children, parents, our job, our self or anything else...then we are walking in holiness. Our love goes beyond feeling. The true test of whether or not we love Jesus this much lies in our obedience to his Word. If we take the time to find out what his Word says and then live it, we are walking in holiness before him.

God's Promise of Healing

Several years ago my husband and I rented a chalet in the mountains of West Virginia for a week. It was completely furnished including sheets, towels and even wood for the fireplace. All we had to bring was our food.

I had been having trouble with my feet—a chronic problem that had been bothering me for a few years to the extent that I could not walk without pain and none of my shoes felt comfortable. Our first morning at the chalet, I asked God to speak to me that very day concerning my feet. I couldn't understand why I had to suffer such a malady and why my prayers for healing went seemingly unanswered.

Later that afternoon I noticed a bookcase at the far end of the living room. Upon examination I found all the books there to be secular except for one tiny paperback by C. S. Lewis entitled, *The Great Divorce*. I opened the book and began to read. It was a story about people who had died and gone to heaven on a bus. As they got off the bus at the outskirts of heaven, they found themselves walking on grass that was so solid it hurt their feet. God lived on top of a mountain. They were required to climb up the mountain to reach God. The closer they came to God, the less the grass hurt their feet.

I knew I had received my answer in a most amazing way. It was clear to me that healing would come gradually as I drew closer to God…and that is exactly what has happened. My feet no longer hurt all the time. I have shoes that are comfortable and most days I can walk all day with no pain. However, I cannot wear the pretty shoes that go with pretty dresses…but then, I haven't reached the top of the mountain.

Most of us think of divine healing as being instantaneous. If we are prayed for and don't see a change in our condition, we believe we weren't healed. God wants to heal us but even more than that, he wants to conform us to the image of Jesus. He desires an intimate relationship with us and out of that intimacy, we will find ourselves being transformed and healed.

I have often wondered how that little book found its way in amongst all those secular books in that mountain chalet. Not only did the book tell about hurting feet being healed, but also it was an allegorical story conveying spiritual truth written by a man who espoused using one's imagination to intuit God—the very essence of what God would be showing me in the four living creatures many years later.

A Word About Healing and Faith

My husband and I have been involved in full Gospel churches for thirty-five years. We have seen countless people prayed for to receive healing for some physical problem yet very few have received a miraculous healing. That is not to say there have been no miracles...there have been. But the vast majority, by far, were not miraculously healed.

From time to time one hears a news story about some Christian family that withheld medicine from their child believing God was healing him, but the child died. We have been taught that if we only believe, we will be healed. Those parents obviously believed and were willing to demonstrate that belief, but the child died. What a terrible tragedy! Those parents were prosecuted and received some retribution as a result of their decision to act on what they had been taught and what they had read in their Bible. This is such a sad thing. Obviously something was lacking in their understanding about healing. It is much more complex than some of the faith teachers teach.

I want to be able to appropriate all of God's promises for my life. I hate being sick and will do anything in my power to not be sick or to be healed if sickness comes upon me. I have searched the scriptures on my own, read books about healing and gone to healing services taught by famous people...Oral Roberts, the Happy Hunters, and Kenneth Hagin to name a few. Things just never worked for me the way these teachers said they should. I'm certain I'm not the only person to discover this.

One teacher taught that healing is just like baking a cake. When you put together certain ingredients, you get a cake. If you did what this teacher said to do, you would get your healing. Well, it just doesn't work like that.

For one thing, God cannot be reduced to a formula. He is Almighty God. He is in charge of each Christian's life. He may be doing an important work through the sickness that is preparing this person for eternity. If the person could be healed by following someone's instructions, the more important eternal work might be thwarted. We are only concerned about our comfort here and now. God knows what we need in our life (which may involve suffering) to prepare us for eternity.

Sickness causes us to move from independence to dependence on God. If we were never weak in our body, some of us would never learn to lean on God. It is through our own weakness that we experience his grace and eventually his strength for our life.

This is a very complex subject, but let me sum it up by saying this: God is in control. If sickness comes into our life, there is some purpose in it for our good if we seek God through it. He may use it to humble us, to get our attention, to point out some sin, to teach us to stand against it through spiritual warfare, to build our faith and myriad other reasons too numerous to list here. However, ultimately God wants us to walk in divine health. That is his goal for us in these end times. We will come into maturity in God and a close relationship with him as we stand against sickness and press into his kingdom as we learn to use parables to come into his presence.

God could heal us every time we ask if he wanted to, but he would be denying us his highest and best. It is a far higher thing to walk with God in oneness of Spirit and allow him to live his life through us. This is the way to divine health where sickness never comes upon us again. To have faith for healing is kindergarten stuff compared to the bride-life of sharing his heart and purpose in oneness of Spirit.

Chapter Five
Moving From the Natural Mind to the Spiritual Mind

Verse Seven - Learning to Control the Imagination
And their feet were straight feet; and the sole of their feet was like the sole of a calf's foot: and they sparkled like the colour of burnished brass.

On the surface, it would appear that verse seven is describing the four living creatures, but actually it is describing the parables. This is still referring to the subject of verse five which was "likeness," meaning "parables."

"Their feet were straight feet." With our feet we walk step-by-step. The only way I can walk from one place to another is by putting one foot ahead of the other over and over again in a series of steps that eventually enable me to go where I desire to be. Forming parables in our mind is like this. We have to work at them over and over again in little steps until they begin to gradually take shape in our mind.

These are straight feet with "straight" meaning "right," "pleasant" and "prosperous." Everything we are using to form these parables will be right, pleasant and prosperous. We are to imagine our self as being perfect. Everything in the vision is to be as perfect as we are able to imagine it to be.

Putting together the above information, our interpretation of the first clause of verse seven reads:

These parables came into being step-by-step (and their feet were) according to what was good, upright, pleasant and prosperous (straight feet).

This is how I made the meadow in my mind. I put it together step-by-step according to all the good and lovely things of earth I could possibly imagine for that setting. As I did so, my body began to respond to the kingdom language of parables. I had tried to claim healing for hay fever many times over the years by quoting scriptures and having faith, but my body didn't understand words. The next clause will give more understanding.

and the sole of their feet was like the sole of a calf's foot:

The word "sole" in Hebrew, *kaph*, can refer to the paw of an animal, the curve of a spoon, or the hollow of a dish. Think of an animal's foot—be it a paw or a hoof. Animals use their paws or hooves to paw at things or dig things up. If they want to get through a door or a fence, they paw at it with their feet. We are like that when we start trying to visualize heavenly things using parables. We are just pawing at the door of the kingdom at first. We make a little indentation like the curve of a spoon or the hollow of a dish. We haven't broken through yet but we are making an indentation.

As I continually returned to the meadow, I began to experience a small breakthrough in my quest for healing of hay fever. I had made an indentation—I was entering a new realm of kingdom health but I still had a ways to go.

In Hebrew, "calf," *'egel*, means "a calf as frisking around, especially one nearly grown."

Our attempt to use our imagination to envision parables is difficult to control at first. Our mind wanders wanting to "frisk around" like a young calf running here and there. We have to keep bringing it back to the thing we are trying to focus upon. It is essential that we not give up when this is happening. If we persevere we will get through this stage. It is like learning anything new…we have to practice. If we do a little each day or a little several times a day, gradually we improve and learn to control our imagination. I believe this is a major step forward into holiness because the imagination seems to have a life of its own. When we learn to control it, we worry less. We don't imagine terrible things happening or entertain ungodly conversations in which we would not actually participate. If we have a concern that the imagination is evil, the best thing we can do is learn to control it because it won't go away and it won't stop functioning.

What we participate in during our day also determines the difficulty or ease with which we control our imagination. If I have watched a movie, my mind will keep returning to scenes from the movie. If I have unforgiveness in my heart towards someone, my mind may tend to gravitate in that direction. The more we clean up our life, the more our imagination will function as we desire it to...in godly visions of our relationship with Jesus.

We read in 1 Pet. 1:13, "...gird up the loins of your mind," or we could say, "gird up the procreative power of your imagination." To "gird" is to "enclose" or "bind up with a belt." We have to continually gird the imagination by bringing it back to our center of focus.

Our spiritual interpretation of "and the sole of their feet was like the sole of a calf's foot" is as follows:

These parables were helping this person break through into the kingdom, but they were much like an animal pawing at a fence in an attempt to reach the other side (and the sole of their feet). This was difficult because their imagination would wander away to other things and then have to be brought back into focus much like a young calf frisking around (was like the sole of a calf's foot).

The final clause of this verse is "and they sparkled like the colour of burnished brass."

"Sparkled," *natsats,* means "to glare," "be bright-colored." According to Webster, "glare," means "to shine with a strong, steady, dazzling light." With parables still being our subject, we see they are becoming stronger, steadier and brighter. Whereas they may have started out as black and white, they are now shining forth in bright colors. All this is because their appearance (colour) has been "burnished."

"Burnished," *qalal,* means "brightened (as if sharpened)," "polished." When we polish or sharpen something we go over it again and again until it reaches the desired sharpness or shine. This is what we do as we rehearse visions of parables in our mind—we go over them again and again until they become strong and steady, no longer frisking around as a calf but "fettered" or "held in check" (brass).

"Brass," *nechosheth,* has an alternate meaning of "fetter." When we fetter something we hold it in check or restrain it. In this verse we have progressed in the use of our imagination for parables from a calf, where our mind frisked around having to be continually brought back to the center of focus, to it being restrained or fettered because of our continual practice.

and the parables were becoming strong, steady and bright (and they sparked) in their appearance (like the colour) because this person rehearsed them in his/her mind over and over again (of burnished) until they were restrained and fettered (brass).

The sum of all of verse seven's interpretations is as follows:

These parables came into being step-by-step (and their feet were) according to what was good, upright, pleasant and prosperous (straight feet). The parables were helping this person break through into the kingdom but they were much like an animal pawing at a fence in an attempt to reach the other side (and the sole of their feet). This was difficult because their imagination would wander away to other things and then have to be brought back into focus much like a young calf frisking around (was like the sole of a calf's foot). And the parables were becoming strong, steady and bright (and they sparked) in their appearance (like the colour) because this person rehearsed them in his/her mind over and over again (of burnished) until they were restrained and fettered (brass).

As this verse reveals, learning to focus on the parables is not easy at first but with practice the imagination learns to maintain its focus. It is like any worthwhile endeavor in life, it requires discipline and practice. No one picks up a musical instrument and just starts playing beautiful music. It takes daily, concentrated effort and discipline to play an instrument well.

When I took my first flute lesson, I became dizzy and thought I might pass out from repeatedly blowing all the air out of my lungs. A few years later, I could comfortably play for hours, but that is because I practiced every day.

Learning to envision parables and focus on them is like learning a new language. We have to practice our new language daily and expand our visions much like we would learn new vocabulary words.

A good place to begin might be to form a lovely scene in your mind. It helps to look at beautiful photographs or landscape paintings such as seen on calendars or in books on art or photography. Find a picture that best conveys a place you would like to be, and then try to commit it to memory. When chaos and terror strike, having a place of safety within where one can experience the presence of Jesus will bring peace.

As we bring Jesus into the lovely setting, we need to determine what he looks like. This was hard for me. I had never particularly cared for artists' pictures of Jesus because I thought no one knew what he looked like. In addition to that, I've never had much of an imagination even as a child. The only thing I knew to do was pick some artist's picture that most appealed to me and begin to imagine Jesus looking like that. It seemed to work well for me and as I have continually expanded my visions, his appearance has become clearer to me. Whether or not this is what he actually looks like is immaterial. At some point further into the revelation of the four living creatures, we will actually see his face but we have to begin somewhere and this seems a good place to start.

Verse Eight - Parables Begin by Earthly Understanding
And they had the hands of a man under their wings on their four sides; and they four had their faces and their wings.

Parables are still the subject here in this verse.

We have already seen the word, "hands," *yad*, in verse three. It means "power and direction."

"Under," *tachath,* means "depressed." "Depressed," according to Webster means, "low in degree," or "suppressed."

"Side," *reba'*, also means "square." Webster defines "square" as: "an instrument used in measuring angles; exact proportion; justness of workmanship and conduct; bring into agreement; etc."

Our understandings of the other words in this verse have been defined elsewhere. Putting these together, our interpretation of verse eight is:

These parables (they) were being empowered and directed (had the hands) by a human being (of a man) whose imagination was of low degree or suppressed (under their wings) because all he understood was about earthly ways (on their four) of measuring, proportioning, bringing things into agreement and judging workmanship (sides). This is because he had a heart (faces) and an imagination (wings) that related only to things of the earth (four).

The meadow I had formed in my mind was of low degree or suppressed in that it was formed according to the standards of the earth rather than heaven. The flowers in my meadow were those of earth—Colorado columbine, Indian paintbrush, buttercups, etc.—those one would expect to see in a typical mountainside meadow. When Jesus and I walked or danced in the meadow, the ground was hard like it is on earth. If we walked on the flowers, they would be crushed under our feet so we walked on paths or in grassy areas. I looked the way I do now with imperfections and the effects of aging visible in my body. Gravity was the same as it is on earth limiting my ability to jump, run or dance.

As I progressed in my ability to use my imagination under the guidance of the Holy Spirit, the meadow changed to a more heavenly or higher perspective.

Verse Nine - Parables become more spiritual
Their wings were joined one to another; they turned not when they went; they went every one straight forward.

In the previous verse we learned that the imagination was of low degree or suppressed. This verse tells us how the imagination begins to rise up to a higher level.

With wings being the imagination, we find that this person has an imagination joined to an imagination. Verse 10 will make all of this much clearer because there we will learn about our two-sided nature. We have a natural side (soul) and a spiritual side (spirit). We have a natural imagination in our soul and we have a spiritual imagination in our spirit. The parables begin through our self-effort in our soul where we labor to form them in our natural imagination. In verse eight we saw that the imagination was of low degree because all it could envision were things concerning the earth in the natural realm of understanding. Now we will see that this natural imagination that labors to make and envision parables is attached to a spiritual imagination that is on a higher level.

Our interpretation of the first clause reveals:

The natural imagination that labored to form the parables according to the standards of the earth was joined to a spiritual imagination in the person (their wings were joined one to anther).

In the next clause, they turned not as they went, the pronoun "they" is referring to the parables. "Turned," *cabab*, means "surround" or "border." Something that is surrounded or has a border is confined within bounds or limits. The parables are no longer confined within bounds of earthly understanding because they "turned not" meaning they no longer had bounds or limitations.

The word "went," *yalak* in Hebrew, means "carry away," "depart," "cause to go away," or "lead forth." These words indicate that these parables are on their way to a destination that is explained in the next clause, they went everyone straight forward.

This word for "straight, *'eber*, means "a region across," and "on the opposite side (espec. of the Jordan)."

"Forward" is the same Hebrew word that was earlier translated as "faces," *paniym*. We have interpreted this to spiritually mean "heart."

Putting all these definitions together we can see that "they went everyone straight forward" means that the parables were crossing over to the other side within the heart. They began through self-effort in the soul or the natural side of the person's heart but they have progressed to the spiritual side where they are no longer confined to the limitations of the natural understanding.

Our spiritual interpretation of verse nine is:

The natural imagination that labored to form the parables according to the standards of the earth was joined to a spiritual imagination in the person (their wings were joined one to another.) Now the parables that were coming forth out of the natural imagination were progressing forward in that they were no longer confined within the bounds and limitations of earthly understanding (they tuned not when they went). This was because they were crossing over from the natural side to the spiritual side in the heart of the person (they went everyone straightforward.)

Remember my example of the meadow I had formed in my mind described in verse six that had been formed according to my natural understanding? The flowers in my meadow were those of earth—Colorado columbine, Indian paintbrush, buttercups, etc.—those one would expect to see in a typical mountainside meadow. When Jesus and I walked or danced in the meadow, the ground was hard like it is on earth. If we walked on the flowers, they would be crushed under our feet, so we walked on paths or in grassy areas. I looked the way I do now with imperfections and the effects of aging visible in my body. Gravity was the same as it is on earth limiting my ability to jump, run or dance.

Gradually this meadow vision began to change and take on more spiritual or heavenly characteristics. Rather than the flowers being like the wildflowers of earth, I began to see larger, more colorful, fragrant flowers unlike any I had seen on earth. The sky was a deeper blue. The little bees flitting from flower to flower sparkled like diamonds in the sun (and, of course, they had no stingers!). I no longer felt heavy as though my body was bound by gravity. I could skip across the tops of the flowers with Jesus without crushing them. My appearance changed from that of an older woman with obvious effects of aging to a beautiful young woman with no imperfections. In these later visions, the bounds of earthly limitations were removed resulting in new freedom to experience Christ in a heavenly dimension. This was because my ability to form parables had progressed from my natural imagination in the soul over to my spiritual imagination.

82

There were other visions too, other lovely places to meet with Jesus that I purposely built step by step in my mind with the Holy Spirit's guidance.

Now that the parables were being generated from my spirit, their healing power increased. My body was responding quicker to the visions. I no longer had to return to them as often for the problem of hay fever because I was being healed. However, there were other physical things that needed healing so we started working on these with other visions. As a result of these visions, other chronic problems were gradually being healed plus I gained the power to resist any sickness that tried to come upon me.

Maybe it was because of allergies, I'm not sure, but it seemed to me that all my life I was susceptible to horrible colds and flu. Others could catch a cold, take some over-the-counter medication and continue on with life. It seemed I was incapacitated by them and that I had more than my share. As a result, I feared sickness. Whenever someone in my household had a cold, I sprayed everything with Lysol, upped my dosage of vitamin C, sucked on zinc lozenges and prayed a lot. I still got sick. The older I got, the more colds I had and the greater their severity.

Jesus began to minister to me for this. The first thing I had to do was die to my fear of sickness. This meant that when someone in my household or my church was sick with a cold or flu, I was to greet them with a handshake, a kiss, or whatever was appropriate and then resist my urge to run to the restroom to wash my hands. Lysol Spray became a thing of the past. I used to cross over to the opposite side of the church from someone hacking and coughing with a chest cold. I learned to approach them without fear and lovingly minister to them.

In addition to this, I had to give up a false belief I had acquired about sickness. All my life I had experienced catching a terrible cold if I went outdoors without a hat on a chilly day. I made sure that every coat I bought had a hood attached because without fail, if I was outdoors in a chilly wind with my head uncovered, I would get sick. The Lord revealed to me that this only happened because I believed it. I had to renounce that lie and allow myself to go hatless on a cold day. I never got sick again from not wearing a hat.

The truth is "what you believe is what you get." We must learn to believe God's Word and renounce the lies of the enemy. If you watch the TV news channels, you'll hear lots of reporting about various diseases, epidemics and warnings about pandemics. They tell us about all the people who died and will die of whatever is going around. Then the commercials kick in advertising all the medicines we need to ask our doctor for when we get this and that malady. We get so inundated with all this, we accept it as inevitable. We need to focus on what God says about our health. We can abide in the secret place of the Most High under the shadow of the Almighty. We need not fear the arrow that flies by day or the pestilence that stalks by night. God gives his angels charge over us lest we dash our foot against a stone. I want to be like Moses of whom at the age of 120 the Bible says, "his eye was not dim and his vigor was not abated."

It has now been thirteen years since I have had a cold or any other kind of sickness. There have been times when a cold tried to come upon me, but I withdrew with Jesus and visualized him healing me in some lovely, heavenly place. Any symptoms of a cold coming on have been mild and they always leave either immediately or in a few days. The awful sickness I used to endure has become a thing of the past. What a joy it is to live free from the fear of sickness!

Parables are stories we make up in our imagination based on Scripture. It is important that they always center in relationship with Jesus. We see these parables as visions in our imagination and power is then released to heal our deepest heart and our physical body. Not only do we find healing through the parables, but also they take us into the presence of Jesus, into the very throne room of God. We go over and over these parables in our mind spending several minutes picturing everything in as much detail as possible repeating them several times during one period of quiet time. I want to include at this point some examples of healing parables I have used that will help the reader understand more about these stories and how they bring healing to our body.

Parable #1 (Based on Ezek. 47 and Rev. 22)

(My problem with painful feet has greatly diminished as a result of God's healing power unleashed through the use of parables. The following is a parable I use often.)

I found myself standing beside Jesus at the edge of the river. Looking up I could see in the distance the glow of the New Jerusalem on a high mountain overlooking the valley. I knew the waters were flowing out from his throne there in that holy city. I also knew there was healing in those living waters for all who were willing to enter in.

On either side of the river were trees—far more beautiful than any trees I had ever seen. The leaves were shimmering in the sunlight with a freshness and vitality that far exceeded ordinary trees on earth. There was power for healing in those trees. The whole setting in which I found myself was conducive to healing and there was indescribable beauty. Fields of flowers stretched out on either side of the river as far as the eye could see—brilliant shades of red, blue, orange, yellow and white.

Jesus sat down by the edge of the river and patted a spot on the grass beside him indicating I was to sit beside him. We sat there together dangling our feet in the refreshing waters without speaking a word for several minutes. I leaned my head upon his chest listening to his heart beat as together we enjoyed the beauty of our surroundings. Presently he gently touched my face and turned it in his direction as he looked deeply into my eyes with such love and compassion it brought tears to my eyes.

"I have brought you here for a reason," he said. "I want to begin healing your feet."

"Oh, Lord, that's awesome!" I replied. "I have desired healing for my feet for so many years!"

"Just think about the healing power in these waters as you keep your feet submerged. I want you to feel the warmth penetrating deep beneath your skin into the muscles and joints of your feet—even into the bones. Imagine your feet changing shape. You know, they are not as I intended. The shoes you wore for so many years kept your toes crammed up and actually changed the shape of your feet. I want you to remember that I created your feet in the first place and it is not difficult for me to erase the effects of earthly wear and tear. Just believe. I want you to return to this place with me as often as you can. Over time you will see a distinct change in the way your feet feel and we will have many hours of sweet fellowship in each other's presence."

I sat there beside him thinking about all he had just said. I was beginning to feel the healing warmth penetrating deeply into my feet—even into the bones. Suddenly Jesus did something that took me completely by surprise. He lifted my feet up out of the water and held them in his lap. Then he reached up and plucked a few leaves from the bough of the tree overhanging the water. Ever so gently he began to massage my feet with the healing leaves in his hands. The gentle movement of his hands and the velvety feel of the leaves were penetrating even deeper into the hurting areas of my feet.

After a while I knew the work was done. I jumped up and raced up and down the bank of the river exclaiming, "Look at me! Look at me! My feet don't hurt anymore. I can run and jump and there is absolutely no pain. This is incredible!"

Jesus immediately arose, grabbed my hands and together we danced and danced over the fields of flowers. I could hear the music of heaven echoing through the valley rejoicing with us in my victory.

Parable #2 (Based on Eph. 3:20)

Jesus and I take a vacation together to Niagara Falls. As we stand arm in arm admiring the beauty and grandeur of the falls, Jesus looks at me and says, "I want you to know, My Beloved, that when I created these spectacular falls I knew there would come a day when the two of us would stand here together enjoying them. I have looked forward to this moment since the creation of the world."

Feeling overwhelmed with his goodness and love for me, the only words I could find to say were, "Thank you. You are so good to me."

He continued on, "Does not my Word say that I am able to do exceeding abundantly above all you could ask or think according to my power that works in you?"

"Yes, Lord, it does," I responded wondering what great truth he wanted me to grasp.

"Look at the power in those falls," he said. "Listen to the roar of the water as it plummets down to the waters beneath. Did you know you have even more power than that within you—a power that is waiting for you to use as you learn to believe my Word?"

"Wow!" I exclaimed. "If only I could believe that. Lord, help my unbelief!"

"My beloved, I want you to picture these falls within yourself. Look at them with the eyes of your imagination and listen to their roar with your spiritual ears. As you do so, new power for healing will be released in your body."

Memorization of Scripture greatly enhances the visions and increases their power. This way, when I am with Jesus, I can talk to him about them and thank him for them. I can even visualize a biblical healing account and put myself into it with a few modifications.

When Jesus first presented the idea of coming to him in my imagination, my motive for coming was to be healed. However, this rapidly changed as I realized how relational the visions were and how quickly they brought me into the Lord's presence and filled my heart with joy and peace.

We read in Prov. 4:23, Keep thy heart with all diligence; for out of it are the issues of life. The Hebrew word for "issues," *towtsa'ah*, means "the place of the exit or termination of anything," "a going out," "geographical boundary," "deliverance," "the place from which (any person or thing) goes forth, hence a gate" (Gesenius).

We will soon understand more fully that our heart is our gate through which we will enter into the kingdom of God. As we continually fill our heart with lovely visions of Jesus and all his glorious truth in parables and pictures, we will be delivered from the pain and suffering of this world. Our heart will be our exit place that will bring termination to our old ways of thinking and the darkness that have held us within the geographical boundaries of earth and the consequences of the fall.

As we continue our study of the four living creatures, we will find that they will take us far beyond mere healing for our bodies. What we have seen thus far is only the beginning. Verse 10 will reveal more about the parables crossing over from the soul side to the spiritual side.

Chapter Six
Our Two-Sided Nature

Verse Ten - Sanctification in Progress

As for the likeness of their faces, they four had the face of a man, and the face of a lion, on the right side: and they four had the face of an ox on the left side; they four also had the face of an eagle.

One of the first things we notice about these people is that they have a right side and a left side. All human beings have a right and a left side. Most of us are right-handed but some are left-handed. This shows us that in the natural, we have one side that is stronger than the other. In the unseen spiritual dimension of life, we also have a left and a right side with one side being stronger than the other.

As Christians, we have a two-sided nature—a carnal nature and a spiritual nature. A carnal Christian lives out of his soul and the spiritual Christian lives out of his spirit. When we were born again unto God, the Spirit of Christ came to dwell in our spirit. It is in the spirit side of our being that we commune with God, intuitively listen for his voice and obey the dictates of our conscience. The soul side of our nature is concerned with things of this world, self-preservation and meeting our needs through our own efforts rather than relying on Christ and trusting in him. One side of our nature will be stronger than the other based on our relationship with Christ and our willingness (or unwillingness) to die to self that Christ may be formed in us.

A brief look at a few scriptures will reveal that our spirit is on our right side and our soul is on our left. This may seem like superfluous information, but actually it is an important concept to be understood for uncovering some deeper spiritual truths God wants to reveal to us.

Eccles. 10:2 reveals, "A wise man's heart is at his right hand; but a fool's heart at his left." A wise Christian is one who lives out of his spirit, being motivated and making decisions based on the communion with Christ that takes place in his spirit on the right side. A foolish or carnal Christian is a person who lives out of his soul making decisions and meeting his needs through his own natural understanding and self-effort apart from Christ on the left side.

Job says, "Behold, I go forward, but he is not there; and backward, but I cannot perceive him: on the left hand, where he doth work, but I cannot behold him: he hideth himself on the right hand, that I cannot see him" (Job 23:8,9). We know that when we are born again, the Holy Spirit comes to reside in our spirit. This is why Job could say that God hides himself on the right side—he dwells in our spirit but we are not able to see him or hear him as we would like.

Job said that God was at work on the left hand. It is in our soul that the work needs to be done. When we live out of our soul, we see life from a human and natural perspective. We strive to fulfill God's mandates and life's basic needs through our own efforts according to our own natural understanding. Because we are basically concerned with self in our soul, all attempts at righteousness having their genesis in the soul will be tainted with impure motives.

Another interesting scripture concerning right and left is found in the New Testament where Jesus said, "Take heed that ye do not your alms before men, to be seen of them: otherwise ye have no reward of your Father which is in heaven. Therefore when thou doest thine alms, do not sound a trumpet before thee, as the hypocrites do in the synagogues and in the streets, that they may have glory of men. Verily I say unto you, they have their reward. But when thou doest alms, let not thy left hand know what thy right hand doeth, that thine alms may be in secret: and thy Father which seeth in secret himself shall reward thee openly" (Matt. 6:1-4).

Jesus was saying here that our giving should spring forth out of our spirit (the right hand) rather than our soul (the left hand). If we give from our spirit, we will be doing so at the unction of the Holy Spirit from a pure and righteous motive; then God will be able to reward us. If we give out of the soul, we will have an impure motive, desiring for others to know about our giving so they can admire and compliment us. The only reward we will receive then is carnal and fleeting. The true rewards come from God in response to our actions that spring forth from our spirit with pure, godly motives.

Let's look at this verse in Ezekiel again:

As for the likeness of their faces, they four had the face of a man, and the face of a lion, on the right side: and they four had the face of an ox on the left side; they four also had the face of an eagle.

We know now that the right side is the spirit side and the left side is the soul side. Faces are still interpreted as hearts. This verse shows the living creatures have four hearts—the heart of a man, the heart of a lion, the heart of an ox and the heart of an eagle.

The Lord promises us that, "...I will give them one heart, and I will put a new spirit within you; and I will take the stony heart out of their flesh, and will give them an heart of flesh" (Ezek. 11:19). If we are to have one heart, then in some way these four hearts must become one heart.

The stony heart is the heart on the left side where our sin nature (flesh) predominates. That heart is concerned for self and cannot appreciate the higher selfless motivations of the heart in the spirit. This is why we feel the battle of these two natures within. God says the stony heart will be removed. We have been taught that our personality and individuality dwell in our soul on the left side—that would be in the stony heart. If that heart is to be removed, what happens to all the characteristics that mark our personhood? The answer is they have to go through the cross; they have to experience death and resurrection whereby they pass from the soul into the spirit. This is the way the stony heart is removed. It passes little by little from the soul side to the spirit side as we yield our will to Christ's. This is our experience if we follow Christ's teaching about the cross as found in Matt. 16:25 and elsewhere, "If any man will come after me, let him deny himself, and take up his cross, and follow me. For whosoever will save his life shall lose it: and whosoever will lose his life for my sake shall find it." The word for "life" here is *psuche* and it means "soul."

Rather than God reaching in and by one action removing the stony heart and putting in a fleshly heart, he takes us through a process—a lifelong process. God is showing us in the four living creatures a picture of sanctification, of working out our salvation with fear and trembling. Different aspects of our life begin in the soul on the left side and, if we are following Christ, will be crucified and resurrected on the other side of our being in the spirit. Thus the stony heart is gradually moved to the other side as it is transformed into a heart of flesh.

For example, every service we perform for God begins in our stony heart mixed with unconscious selfish motives and self-effort. No matter how much we love God and want to serve him, our early efforts at ministry begin in our soul. The ministry must suffer some type of death experience or yielding of the will and then pass into the spirit to be empowered by God.

One example may be found in the testimony I once heard about a well-known gospel singer. He had been blessed with a beautiful voice that he used for blessing God and others. But there came a day when that wonderful ministry had to go to the cross. He lost his voice for a period of time not knowing if he would ever sing again. During that ordeal, he died to the ministry by humbly submitting it all to God and conceding that if he never sang again, he would still love God and walk in the joy of knowing Christ. Once God determined that he had died to the ministry, he gave him back his voice. The ministry then took on a whole new dimension of spiritual power and anointing. What had once come forth from the soul was purified and now coming from the spirit where it was empowered by Christ's Spirit.

The parables are like this. They begin on the left side in our soul through our own self-effort with mixed motives. I first began envisioning parables because God told me to (a righteous motive) and also to gain healing for my body (not an evil motive, but not the highest either). But it wasn't long before I envisioned them in order to come into the Lord's presence and enjoy being with him (a higher spiritual motive). At first they were difficult to envision because I was laboring to make them by my own efforts, but soon I experienced greater ease and more power in the parables because they were generated more from my spirit than from my soul.

Parables have greater power and ease of formation from the spiritual heart on the right side because that heart is joined with the heart of Jesus Christ. Jesus is the Lion of the tribe of Judah in

Rev. 5:5. Therefore the face (heart) of a lion is referring to the heart of Christ. These hearts are united being one in purpose with pure motives and empowered by God.

To restate, verse 10 speaks of four faces or rather four hearts. There are the heart of the person and the heart of a lion (Christ) on the right side in the spirit. The heart of an ox is on the left side. The ox, being a beast of burden, is a symbol of labor. We labor by our own efforts in our soul on the left side. So the face of the ox is the stony heart of the soul. The heart of the eagle is not said to be on either side so its importance is not related to "place" but to "function" as will be seen. Somehow, these four hearts must become one heart because God said he would give us one heart.

The heart of man joined with the heart of Christ in the spirit has become one heart in total unity. The remaining unregenerate heart of the soul (ox) that has not passed through the cross into the spirit will eventually be severed and removed. At that point we will enter into complete rest in Christ.

It would be helpful to think of the spirit gradually becoming larger as the purified soul passes over into it. The small, unregenerate part of the soul that is left will be severed and removed. If we have consistently embraced the cross, there will be very little remaining in the soul side of our being.

In Ezekiel 1 the four living creatures have the face of an ox. In Ezekiel 10 the face of an ox has become the face of a cherub. This is because the unregenerate soul, the part of man filled with self that keeps him earth bound, has been removed. The place where the soul has been will be filled with a powerful new dimension of the spirit. At this point, the living creatures will be as Christ was after his resurrection.

Further evidence that the remaining part of the soul will be removed can be seen in the words used for "living creature" in Ezekiel. These words are different in Ezekiel than anywhere else in Scripture. The words, "living creature" are also found in Genesis and Leviticus where the Hebrew words are "*chay nephesh*," which actually mean "living soul." In the KJV of the Bible, "*chay nephesh*" is translated "living creature" eight times, "living thing" once and "living soul" once.

They are translated "living soul" in Gen. 2:7 where we read, "And the LORD God formed man of the dust of the ground, and breathed into his nostrils the breath of life; and man became a living soul (*chay nephesh*).

We have established that the living creatures are mature Christians living in the end times; however, they are not referred to as *chay nephesh* or "living souls." They are *chay chay*. There is no word for soul used here and this is the only place in the Bible where *chay chay* is used. The meaning is obvious. These words *chay chay* are prophetically showing that in order to come into the glorified state where one is as Christ after his resurrection, there can be no soul in the unregenerate state. The soul is saved as it passes through the cross where the sin is torn away and the purified portion of the soul passes into the spirit in the process of death and resurrection. This is how we work out our salvation with fear and trembling. This is why we will lose our soul if we refuse to suffer with Christ. "He that loveth his life (*psuche*/soul) shall lose it; and he that hateth his life (*psuche*/soul) in this world shall keep it unto life eternal" (John 12:25). This is why the description of the four living creatures in Ezekiel 10 omits the face of an ox but adds the face of a cherub.

The temporality of the soul and the eternal nature of the spirit are also seen in Strong's definition of soul in the Greek:

Soul - 5590. *psuche, psoo-khay'*; from G5594; breath, i.e. (by impl.) spirit, abstr. or concr. (the animal sentient principle only; thus distinguished on the one hand from G4151, which is the rational and immortal soul; and on the other from G2222, which is mere vitality, even of plants: these terms thus exactly correspond respectively to the Heb. H5315, H7307 and H2416):—heart (+ -ily), life, mind, soul, + us, + you.

Notice that soul, *psuche*, is the animal sentient principle only. It is distinguished (different and separate from) G4151, *pneuma*, which is translated "spirit," "life," "ghost" or "mind." *Pneuma* is the rational and immortal soul. Therefore, *psuche* (soul) is not the immortal soul. Only after the soul passes through the cross into the spirit does it become the immortal soul.

Of the four hearts mentioned in Ezek. 1:10, we have established that the two hearts on the right side in the spirit are united as one. The heart on the left side in the soul will be severed and discarded. That leaves one more heart—the heart (face) of an eagle.

Strong's definition for "eagle," *nesher,* is from an unused root meaning "to lacerate." Webster says "lacerate" means "to tear," and "to wound or hurt." The eagle has a sharp beak with which he tears flesh away from dead animals. I stated earlier that the soul is saved as it passes through the cross where the sin nature is torn away and the purified portion of the soul passes into the spirit in the process of death and resurrection. This is what the heart of an eagle shows us. Rather than an actual heart (it is not given a location as are the other three hearts), it is a function of the spiritual heart. It shows the process we endure when we are willing to suffer for the sake of Christ. Our will, along with our understanding, personality and works of service are formed in the soul with mixed motives, some pure and some impure. These various qualities of our soul are taken through a process by the Holy Spirit whereby the sin nature is torn away (lacerated) from the aspect of the soul being sanctified. The sanctified part of the soul rises up on eagles' wings as it passes in purified state into the spirit. There will come a time when the heart of an eagle, meaning the process of tearing away the flesh, will no longer be needed for this individual himself. However, this function will again be used for others in the great end time ministry of the four living creatures seen in Ezekiel 10. At this point, there will be one heart—the spiritual heart of man united with the heart of Christ in the spirit. The unregenerate heart of the soul will have been removed. The heart of the eagle is viewed as a function rather than an actual heart (or it could be seen as the heart in process that is only in this state for a brief period of time). When this process is completed, we will be as Christ was after his resurrection. He was able to appear or disappear yet his disciples could touch him.

And as they thus spake, Jesus himself stood in the midst of them, and saith unto them, Peace be unto you. But they were terrified and affrighted, and supposed that they had seen a spirit. And he said unto them, Why are ye troubled? and why do thoughts arise in your hearts? Behold my hands and my feet, that it is I myself: handle me, and see; for a spirit hath not flesh and bones, as ye see me have. And when he had thus spoken, he showed them his hands and his feet. And while they yet believed not for joy, and wondered, he said unto them, Have ye here any meat? And they gave him a piece of a broiled fish, and of an honeycomb. And he took it, and did eat before them (Luke 24:36-43).

By way of review, we see the soul laboring on its own in verses 6 through 8. Then the spirit comes into action in verse 9.

In verse six, we learned that the parables were coming forth from hearts and imaginations that only understood about earthly things. This is clearly speaking of the soul.

In verse seven, the parables were growing steadier and brighter as these persons went over them again and again in their mind. This is the self-effort of the soul, a necessary process before they can pass into the spirit because we must labor to enter into rest.

In verse eight, we learned that the parables were still being formed by an imagination that was of low degree in that it only understood earthly things. Again this is definitely referring to the soul.

In verse nine, we learned that the imagination in the soul was joined to another imagination, the spiritual imagination. Let's look at that verse again:

Their wings were joined one to another; they turned not when they went; they went every one straight forward.

Here we see the spirit being activated to transport the parables, or rather the ability to form parables from the soul side over to the spiritual side of the person. Before this verse, the parables were formed solely by the person's self-effort in the soul. There is no mention of anything of the spirit involved in the making of parables prior to this verse. The spirit transporting the parables to the other side is the spirit of the person joined with the spirit of Christ because "he that is joined unto the Lord is one spirit." (1 Cor. 6:17).

To restate our spiritual interpretation of verse nine:

The natural imagination that labored to form the parables according to the standards of the earth was joined to a spiritual imagination in the person (their wings were joined one to another.) Now the parables that were coming forth out of the natural imagination were progressing forward in that they were no longer confined within the bounds and limitations of earthly understanding (they tuned not when they went). This was because they were crossing over from the natural side to the spiritual side in the heart of the person (they went everyone straight forward.)

Here in Ezekiel 1 we are seeing in the parables an example of a process that has been ongoing in the life of a committed believer. Every Christian should be experiencing this transformational process by daily choosing to deny himself, take up his cross and follow Christ. The following will be our word-for-word spiritual interpretation of the first part of verse 10:

As for the likeness of their faces, they four had the face of a man, and the face of a lion, on the right side: And they four had the face of an ox on the left side;

As always, "likeness" means "parables," and "faces" are "hearts." Once again the subject of this verse is parables.

Four is the number meaning creative works.

As for the parables (as for the likeness) of their hearts (of their faces), some of these parables (they) were being created (four) from the heart (face) of a man joined with the heart (face) of Christ (lion) in their spirit (on the right side). Other parables (they) were being created (four) from a heart (had the face) that labored to form them by its own human effort apart from Christ (of an ox) on the carnal, soul side (on the left side).

There is a time of transition as the parables are passing from the soul to the spirit when they are coming forth from both sides. However, this does not last long because of the work of the "eagle."

The final clause of this verse states:

they four also had the face of an eagle

As we stated before, the Hebrew word for eagle, *nesher,* is from an unused root meaning, "to lacerate." According to Webster, "lacerate" means "to tear, to rend, to separate a substance by violence or tearing; as to lacerate the flesh. It is applied chiefly to the flesh or figuratively to the heart."
The subject here is still parables.

These parables (they) were accomplishing the creative work (four) of tearing away the flesh by separating the stony heart of the soul from the spiritual heart in the spirit (the face of an eagle).

One by one various aspects of the soulish heart that are joined to the heart of the spirit are transported into the spirit while the flesh is torn away. This tearing away of the soul or flesh from the spirit (the heart in process) is revealed to be the face (heart) of an eagle.

When we focus our mind on spiritual truth in the form of parables seen in the imagination, the Holy Spirit works in us to separate flesh (sin nature) from the part of the soul being purified and transports the purified soul into the spirit. This, as stated earlier, has been an ongoing process in the life of the believer, but the parables greatly facilitate and expedite this process.

As various aspects of the soul are torn away from the flesh and transported into the spirit, the soul side of our being gradually becomes weaker and smaller. Each time we go through this process, one layer of the veil of our flesh that separates us from Christ is removed. The New Testament speaks of this veil in 2 Cor. 3:14-16, "But their minds were blinded: for until this day remaineth the same veil untaken away in the reading of the old testament; which veil is done away in Christ. But even unto this day, when Moses is read, the veil is upon their heart. Nevertheless when it shall turn to the Lord, the veil shall be taken away."

This passage is referring to the Jews who rejected Christ. However, we also have a veil over our heart. As our soul turns to the Lord one aspect at a time, a layer of the veil is removed (or we could say, veils are removed, with each layer being a veil).

Perhaps this can be seen more clearly if we briefly look at an Old Testament type—the Tabernacle of Moses. This tabernacle was built according to an exact pattern given to Moses by God. It consisted of three basic sections—the outer court, the Holy Place and the Holy of Holies. These three divisions have been interpreted spiritually as referring to (among other things) the three aspects of our tripartite humanity: the outer court being the physical body, the Holy Place being the soul and the Holy of Holies typifying the spirit.

All Israelites could see the outer court just as our physical body is visible to all. Only the priests could enter into the Holy Place, and we alone have access to our soul. The Holy of Holies where God dwelled could only be accessed once a year and only by the High Priest on the Day of Atonement. In order to enter the Holy of Holies, he had to go through an elaborate purification process and then pass through a thick veil described by some as being about four inches thick. This veil is a type of the veil of our flesh. This veil in us is very thick and God removes it layer by layer. As each layer is removed, the veil becomes thinner until at some point, the veil will be completely removed and the spirit will totally fill the area that used to be the soul. When Christ died, this veil (which was later in the temple) was torn from top to bottom by God. Each time we die to self, God tears away a veil of our flesh that separates us from his presence in our spirit (the Holy of Holies).

Our soul and spirit are connected. We know this because Heb. 4:12 states that the word of God separates the soul and spirit. As we established, the spirit is on the right side and the soul is on the left. The place where they are joined is called the veil. This veil blocks our access to the things of the spirit making it difficult to hear the Lord's voice or sense his presence. Each time something passes through the cross from our soul into our spirit, one layer of this veil is removed. This veil is very thick in an immature Christian. Therefore, he lives out of his soul with very little comprehension of his spirit because it is hidden behind this thick veil or curtain. In mature Christians who have been willing to join in the fellowship of the sufferings of Christ, the veil has become thin. When the veil is thin, we are able to access the things of the spirit. We become sensitive to the Lord's voice. We receive revelation when we study his Word. The Lord is able to pour out his love and presence through us to others as there is very little of the veil left to block the flow of his Spirit. Through the sufferings of the cross, our will has become one with his will and his life has become our life. We enter into his rest as seen below:

There remaineth therefore a rest to the people of God. For he that is entered into his rest, he also hath ceased from his own works, as God did from his. Let us labour therefore to enter into that rest, lest any man fall after the same example of unbelief. For the word of God is quick, and powerful, and sharper than any twoedged sword, piercing even to the dividing asunder of soul and spirit, and of the joints and marrow, and is a discerner of the thoughts and intents of the heart (Heb. 4:9-12).

It is God's plan that we cease from our own works and enter into the rest of God. What a paradox that we must labor in order to rest, but God has made it so. In verse 10 of Ezekiel 1 we are shown how man enters into that rest. The ox, or soul, is torn away. That part of us that labors to do God's will by our own efforts is separated from the spiritual side enabling us to cease doing our own works and allow the spirit to soar with Christ as an eagle and enter into his rest. Forming parables in the soul seems like hard work. Once this ability has progressed over to the spirit side, they come forth with ease.

The parables coming forth in pure form from the spirit side are actually the word of God in parabolic form. Jesus is the same yesterday, today and forever. He spoke in parables when he walked on the earth in human flesh and he continues to speak to us in parables from heaven in the spirit side of our being. These words from God are separating the soul from the spirit. At this stage of development, these mature Christians are able to experience the removal of layers of the veil, not necessarily through painful cross experiences because they have died to almost everything of this world, but the remaining veils are removed as we spend time in the Lord's presence, loving him, receiving his love and visualizing the parables.

When we purposefully spend time each day visualizing the face of God while personally relating with him in a beautiful heavenly setting created in our mind, the Holy Spirit is activated to move aspects of our being from the soul over to the spirit and remove layers of the veil from our heart.

Here is an example of a parable seen as a vision created in an imagination inspired by the Holy Spirit that can help lift a person into a higher level of spiritual development with Jesus:

Parable #3

I ran down the pathway through the dark, thick woods as fast as I could. The light from the garden up ahead was warm and inviting because Jesus was waiting for me there. As always, the look of love and delight on his face upon seeing me caused me to fall more deeply in love with him. As I ran into his arms, he held me closely for a few minutes and then we walked hand in hand around the garden admiring the lovely flowers and fountains until we came to a crystal clear pond. The surface was stretched out before us like a sheet of glass without even a ripple. The Lord indicated that if we looked down into the water we might see some fish. As we peered over the side to look, I lost any interest in fish because of something else I saw that astounded and thrilled me. In the still surface of the pond, I saw our two faces reflected as in a mirror. That in itself is not what delighted me so—it was the realization of how alike we looked! I still looked like myself and Jesus looked like himself, and yet we were alike as though we had become one.

Jesus said, "Yes, you are growing more like me every day. There will come a time soon when people will look at you and see only me."

Over to our left near the pond was a tree covered with fragrant pink blossoms. Hanging from the bough of the tree was a swing—something like a porch swing with a back on it where people could lean back and relax while admiring the beauty and serenity of the garden. We sat there and talked for a while as I shared with him the events of my day and some other things that were on my mind.

While looking into his face and talking, I lost all sense of our surroundings, but suddenly I realized we were no longer in the garden. Looking up I could see the swing was not actually tied to a bough of the tree but the ropes that held it were anchored somewhere high in the sky out of my sight. Entwined around the entire length of each rope were colorful flowers and green ferns lovely beyond description. We were swinging higher and higher. Soon we were swinging out over mountaintops, and even the ocean, as we looked down on the earth from breathtaking height.

Jesus put his arms around me and said, "Do not fear, my beloved. I am taking you to a new level." The next thing I knew, we had catapulted from the swing and were flying through the air towards a fluffy white cloud nearby. As we entered the cloud, I realized he was taking me through a veil. Our feet landed on something soft but substantial, and we entered into a new land of indescribable beauty.

The following is our complete spiritual interpretation of verse 10:

As for the parables (as for the likeness) of their hearts (of their faces), some of these parables were being created (they four) from the heart of a man joined with the heart of Christ (had the face of a man and the face of a lion) in their spirit (on the right side). Other parables (they) were being created (four) from a heart (face) that labored to form them by its own human effort apart from Christ (ox) on the carnal, soul side (on the left side). The parables (they) were accomplishing the creative work (four) of tearing away the flesh by separating the carnal heart from the spiritual heart (the face of an eagle).

Chapter Seven
Rising Up in Spirit

Verse Eleven - Our Two Bodies
Thus were their faces: and their wings were stretched upward; two wings of every one were joined one to another, and two covered their bodies.

The beginning of verse 11 seems to summarize what we have learned previously about the hearts when it states, "thus were their faces (hearts)." In verse 10 we saw the ability to create parables crossing over into the spiritual heart and severed from the soul as a veil of flesh was removed. The ability to create parables is a function of our imagination, so the imagination as it functions to create parables has become part of the spirit. Now in verse 11 we will see the results of that transformation.

And their wings were stretched upward;

"Wings," of course, are still the imagination.
"Stretched," *parad*, means "to break through" and "to separate."
"Upward," *ma'al*, means "above" and "very high" from the root word, *'alah*, meaning "the upper part."

And the imagination (and their wings) was breaking through into a very high place in the realm of the spirit because it had been separated from the soul that had kept it earthbound (were stretched upward).

We saw in verse nine that when the ability to envision parables was crossing over to the spiritual side, they were no longer limited by earthly understandings but had a more heavenly spiritual perspective. We shall see here in verse 11 that not only has the ability to form the parables become more spiritual but there is a new dimension of spirit being added. Our examination of the rest of this verse will disclose what this new dimension is.

Two wings of every one were joined one to another

Here in verse 11 the number "two" is introduced for the first time in this Ezekiel passage. We must remember our guideline for spiritual interpretation designates that numbers are not for disclosing "how many" but for revealing their spiritual meaning. The number "two" means division or difference. The second of any number of things always bears upon it the stamp of difference, and generally of enmity.

Take the second statement in the Bible. The first is, Gen. 1:6: "In the beginning God created the heaven and the earth."

The second is, "And the earth was (or rather became) without form and void."

Here the first speaks of perfection and of order. The second of ruin and desolation, which came to pass at some time, and in some way, and for some reason which is not revealed.

Now that we have learned the meaning of "two," let's look at this verse again.

Two wings of every one were joined one to another.

The word "wings" is not in the original Hebrew but was added by the translators for ease of reading. It should really read:

Two of every one were joined one to another.

There is no indication yet as to what these two things are, but putting together what we now know about this clause we can interpret it as meaning:

There were two entities that were joined together (every one were joined one to another). These two entities were different from one another with one being more perfect and the other being lower and subject to ruin and desolation (two).

We know the two entities that are joined cannot be the hearts or the imaginations because these have been separated.

104

These two entities have to be something else. The last clause of this verse will reveal what these two joined entities are:

and two covered their bodies.

"Covered," according to Webster means, "to place something on, over, or in place of, so as to conceal, protect or close.

The entity alluded to in the previous clause about two things being joined together with one being perfect and the other being subject to corruption is revealed here to be bodies. We have two bodies, a natural body and a spiritual body (1 Cor. 15:44b). The spiritual body is higher and perfect. The physical body is lower as a result of the fall and subject to death and decay. There is a covering in that one is placed over the other thereby concealing the one underneath. Now our spiritual interpretation for verse 11 in its entirety reads:

As the spiritual heart was being separated from the natural heart (thus were their hearts), the imagination (their wings) was breaking through (stretched) to a very high place above (upward). There were two entities that were joined together (every one were joined one to another). These two entities were different from one another with one being perfect and the other being lower and subject to corruption (two). These entities were the natural body and the spiritual body. There was a covering in that one body [the natural body] was placed over the other body [the spiritual body] so that the spiritual body was concealed (and two covered their bodies).

The new dimension of spirit that comes after the imagination is severed from the soul concerns the spiritual body. Our spiritual body has been within us but dormant waiting to be activated upon our death when the physical body is left behind. However, in these end times when it is time for this mortal to put on immortality, death, our last enemy, will be destroyed. The four living creatures will be revealing that before this mortal puts on immortality, we must first be taken by God through a process. Part of this process concerns our spiritual body.

The Spiritual Body - My Experience

In 1996 my husband and I were asked to pastor the Rochester, NY Foursquare Church. We moved from Newark, Ohio to Rochester with everything we owned in a U-Haul truck in a snow storm in January. When we arrived at the parsonage that night, there were several people from the church waiting there to greet us and help unload the truck. One of those persons was a woman named Brenda.

We had not been at our new church more than a few weeks before I began to notice that Brenda had some severe emotional problems that I recognized as being the result of extreme childhood abuse. Years previously the Lord had called me to minister to severely abused women, and I had learned to recognize the symptoms of such abuse.

Brenda and her husband had been at the church for over twenty years, and they never missed a meeting. It was not long before Brenda and I became good friends, and she began to confide in me about things she had never told anyone. Due to the anointing God has placed on my life that seems to happen to me a lot. Women just open up and start pouring out their heart. It was a little different with Brenda. Every time she came around me, she started to cry and sort of "fall apart." It was like she didn't have any choice about this…it just happened. I began ministering to her on a regular basis, and before long she was having memories of the most severe abuse imaginable.

In April of that first year in Rochester, some of the women of our church attended a women's retreat in Buffalo. Brenda and I shared a room. Our first morning there, we were both up early having our private time of prayer and devotion. I was sitting at a desk with my back to Brenda. She was sitting on the bed. I was praying silently and asking God to give me a double anointing of his Spirit.

At the exact moment I was praying for this silently, Brenda spoke up saying she had just had a vision. She saw the Lord coming to me and placing two cloaks on me. One was red symbolizing his love and the other was purple representing his power and authority. I had never spoken to her or anyone about wanting a double anointing.

This was the beginning of a very unique ministering relationship where I ministered to her for her abuse and she would have a vision or prophetic word for me at the end of each ministry session. Her abuse was so extremely severe that we met everyday for years. There was so much to deal with and she was so broken there was no other way. The Lord kept saying, "The time is short." So...I received many, many visions and prophetic words. I have stacks of notebooks and tape recordings full of words from God. It soon became evident that she was God's instrument for leading me through the veils into his presence. It is interesting that before we met, she had no idea she had a prophetic gifting.

In addition to the prophetic words and visions from Brenda, I spent several hours every morning in prayer and Bible study. This book on the four living creatures is a result of those studies. God never used Brenda to tell me where to study or what I would find in his Word. She did, however, offer a lot of encouragement.

Some may ask, why would God use a woman so broken to do this ministry? It was precisely her brokenness that enabled her to minister so mightily to me. When little children suffer so greatly, Jesus comes to them and helps them in many ways. At least, this has been the experience of several of the women to whom I have ministered over the past twenty-two years. Brenda's abuse was the worst of anyone I have known and therefore, the veil was the most open.

The veil was also open because she had learned to use her imagination in order to survive. When she was locked in a room for days at a time, she imagined she was outside playing with her friends. Her family was so unbearably wicked, she began to imagine they were really good people. She had a phenomenal ability to dissociate...to split from the mainstream of consciousness and form another so-called identity. In this way she could completely forget what her life was really like and pretend it was something else. This fascinated her abusers, so they abused her all the more to see how quickly and thoroughly she could forget.

Brenda could see, hear, smell, and feel things I could not. During times of ministry, she was able to see into heaven, see the Lord and sometimes smell his fragrance. She could also hear him speak. As I observed her and studied the Word, I came to the conclusion that she could experience these things because her spiritual body had been awakened. Mine was asleep. According to 1 Cor. 15: 44, "There is a natural body, and there is a spiritual body." I was content to be as I was. I knew she had these abilities because of her horrendous abuse. However, I also believed there would come a time in the end times, when Jesus would awaken the spiritual bodies of believers, but I had no idea when that would be or how it would happen.

In February of 1997, about a year after I had started ministering to Brenda (and she to me), she had a vision of Jesus and me together in a lovely meadow. We were sitting on a large rock talking. Jesus reached down and touched my feet and said, "These feet will never touch the earth again." I had no idea what that meant.

That night as I was lying in bed all relaxed and waiting for sleep to come, I began to feel a very pleasant and rhythmic tingling sensation in my feet that worked its way up my legs and spread out over my entire body. I immediately related it to the vision earlier that day where Jesus touched my feet and said they would never touch the earth again. Now I knew he was not speaking of my natural feet but of my spiritual feet. My spiritual body was being awakened. It was a distinct, personal and most wonderful experience which is difficult to describe. The feeling has never left but has only intensified. Because this is a spiritual experience, it is difficult to describe in words. Now I understand why so much of the Bible is written as allegory. There would be no other way to explain spiritual things except by relating them to natural things we understand.

I will attempt to describe the feeling of the spiritual body being awakened by Jesus. It is a very gentle, slow rhythmic feeling almost like a deep massage but it doesn't touch the skin. It is deep inside and it gives the feeling of being deeply loved. Every fiber of my being feels loved. It is like bobbing up and down on a raft resting upon gentle waves like one would experience in a bay perhaps. Ocean waves would be too strong. These are gentle waves. They never, ever stop...not for one second. I cannot tell my physical body from my spiritual body because my whole being feels this wonderful sense of God's love and quickening. It is deeply relaxing and comforting.

I know I am never alone because I am able to feel God's love at all times. It is a most wonderful and amazing experience and a necessary one for what we are about to experience as the Antichrist spirit begins to attempt to take over the world. No matter what is going on around us, this knowledge that we are loved and we are not alone never leaves.

It also brings an understanding that we have entered into the supernatural realm. Things will never be the same. Part of us has risen above the earthly realm and heaven is very near. This is the realm we will need to live in as our world crumbles around us.

We know by this event that we are in the end times. This is not something experienced by the saints of bygone years. This is a new experience and one reserved for this particular time in history. It is part of the events of the return of Jesus for his bride. God never does things the way we think he will. This experience came as a total surprise to me.

At this point I think it is important to state what this is not. It is not a floating out away from the body kind of kooky weird-spirit thing. I don't hear voices or see spirits. I don't float up to the ceiling and look down and see myself. No! That is definitely not what I am describing here. It is a quickening…an awakening of something that has been asleep since the fall. Only Jesus can do this in us. It is an individual and personal experience that was reserved for the church of the end times.

More about Parables

As Jesus works in us to perfect our body, we need to focus on heavenly things with our mind. In most instances we don't need to visualize the work he is doing as he transforms our bodies, we just need to focus on HIM and our relationship with him in a more spiritual and heavenly realm. The parables I am writing for this book are only suggestions to help others understand the type of parables Jesus wants to encourage us to visualize. Since each person is different, Jesus will be seen in our imagination according to our perception of him. Some will see him as friend, some as father, others as bridegroom, etc. Whatever our perception of him, we all need to grow in our understanding of his love. It is far greater than anything we have ever known or imagined. Many of us tend to keep him distant, seated on a throne as he judges everything we do. Yes, he is on the throne in the sense that he is the authority over all things, and yes, we must give account for our every thought and action, but his love is over all, in all and through all the whole reason we even exist. His love is what motivates everything he does. He is not far away. He is closer than the air we breathe. He created us to love and our purpose for living is to experience that love and return to him all of our love.

I am reminded of a song I've been listening to a lot lately from a CD by Phillips, Craig and Dean. The words begin with the singer wondering if there is any way to express his love to the Lord. He comes up with the following words that present a picture of pouring out his love:

Like oil upon your feet
Like wine for you to drink
Like water from my heart
I pour my love on you
If praise is like perfume
I'll lavish mine on you
Till every drop is gone
I'll pour my love on you. (Dean and Sadler)

There are many ideas in the words of this song for how we might visualize loving Jesus. As we will learn further on in the four living creatures, the spiritual dynamics of this kind of visualizing go far beyond imagination. Jesus feels our touch as we use our imagination to lavish our love upon him. We will also learn that we will begin to feel in our body, his touch and his love as he pours it out on us.

Even though Jesus is fully God, he is also fully man—the most loving man who ever lived. He longs to be close to his people. He wants to fill us with himself. He wants to demonstrate his love to us and we need to visualize him in order to understand and receive a fuller dimension of this love. God is spirit; however, I can't visualize spirit, but I can visualize a man and I can visualize the way he would reveal his love to me.

Parable #4 (Based on John 17:26 and 2 Kings 4:32-35)

Jesus entered my bedroom after I had retired for the day. He said, "I'm glad you got to bed earlier tonight. There is much I want to do with you before you fall asleep. I so look forward to our evening times together when there are no interruptions and I can have your full attention."

"Yes, so do I," I responded, "but right now my mind is racing with the events of the day."

"Tell me about your day," Jesus said.

I began to talk over with him everything that happened that day and how I felt about each event.

"You know," Jesus responded, "I will take care of all things if you will just rest and release them to me."

"Yes, my head knows this," I lamented, "but my heart is a little slow to respond."

"I'll help you," Jesus said, as he placed before me a huge empty box. "Put everything in here, and we'll think about these things tomorrow—and remember, I am working on them."

Then in my mind I formed a picture of each concern and handed it to Jesus as he put each one in the box. Then he placed the box up on a high shelf and it vanished from my sight.

"Now, my Darling," he lovingly said, "you have made room for me to fill you with more of myself which is exactly what I want to do tonight."

He lifted me into his arms and we rose up in the air much like a hummingbird I had seen earlier that day that drank from our feeder and then shot up in the air like a jet aircraft. Unlike a jet, there was no sensation of air being forced against my body or of "pulling G's," but just a gentle floating up into the atmosphere above the earth where we lighted upon a fluffy white cloud.

The sun had sunk down below the horizon in a blaze of glory and now darkness engulfed the earth. We were peering over the edge of the cloud looking at the spectacular lights of the cities and town below.

"Aren't the lights just gorgeous!" I exclaimed.

"Yes, he agreed, "but not so lovely as the light I see in your eyes when you look at me. Your love for me is growing stronger and more perfect every day. I see you turning away from the things of this world as the knowledge that I am all you need grows in you. Tonight I want to fill you with more of myself."

"That is truly my heart's desire!" I exclaimed with delight and anticipation.

Then Jesus began to teach me from the Old Testament. "There are many things hidden beneath the surface of my Word in the stories about Elisha that pertain to these end times," he said. "The truths behind many of these accounts that have puzzled my people for centuries will now be revealed because they will help prepare my people for events soon to engulf the world."

"That is very exciting," I said with anticipation mingled with apprehension. I knew as these events unfolded, life would become more difficult and our faith would be challenged.

Jesus continued, "Do you remember the account of the Great Woman of Shunem who, at the word of Elisha, miraculously conceived a son who later died?"

"Yes, Lord, I do. I studied that story in great detail."

"Then you will recall how Elisha stretched his body over the body of the dead child and the child was revived."

"Yes," I replied.

Jesus continued, "His mouth was upon the child's mouth, his eyes upon his eyes, and his hands upon his hands. That is one of the ways I will come upon my people in these end times. As they visualize being with me, I will be overshadowing them and sinking into them to fill them with the power, love and wisdom they will need for these difficult times. I want you to lie here on this soft cloud and let me fill you with more of myself. I am able to do this only because you have been emptying yourself of the things of this earth that used to fill you."

As I lay upon the cloud, my whole body was tingling with anticipation of what was about to transpire. It was hard to believe this wonderful thing was actually happening to me! Soon I was aware of his Spirit coming down upon my whole body ever so gently—the feeling was much like a warm blanket gently falling, falling, falling as softly as a down feather. The sensation was very slight yet fully perceptible. I held my breath as long as possible so I could feel the fullness of the wonder of this tender moment. "If only I didn't have to breathe," I thought. The experience was so gentle that the very act of breathing seemed to lessen my perception of it. It wasn't long before I had fallen into a deep sleep.

The next morning I wondered how I could have fallen asleep when something so wonderful was happening. I felt the Lord saying, "You were tired and needed your rest. We will pick up tonight where we left off last night."

Chapter Eight
Leaving Behind the Shackles of Human Frailty

Our natural bodies are going to have to be changed if we are to survive the destructive forces coming forth from those who are in league with the Devil for ushering in the New World Order. There are powerful people in high places of influence and government all over the world who believe there are too many people on this earth and it would be a good idea to eliminate a few billion of them. The easiest way to do this is to attack the food supply.

This is being done in many ways. Just one way is by teaching in our universities and elsewhere that farmers are ruining the earth with their tilling of the land that results in destroying the natural habitat of animals. Our cabin in the mountains of New York overlooks a cornfield where we regularly see wild animals benefitting from the cornfield's presence. Turkeys meander through every day eating the corn that raccoons or bears have left behind from their feast of corn from previous days. This particular farmer also raises beef cattle, and we buy our meat from him. Of course, raising beef has now become politically incorrect because the methane gas given off by cows is reputed to be destroying the earth by contributing to "global warming."

Already we have seen the contamination of our food with e-coli and salmonella...a problem which will only increase because we will have to import more of our food supply from foreign nations due to our decrease in productivity. For example, farmers in California have not been allowed to irrigate their crops because taking the water from the Delta where two big rivers join is causing the smelt there, an endangered species, to disappear. A federal judge ruled that the amount of water being delivered from that area to the farmers had to be sharply curtailed. As a result, farmers are losing their crops and their farms. One almond orchard had to have one third of its almond trees, which had been cultivated for over thirty years, cut down because of lack of water. In order to save this one fish, a far larger source of food from the farms along with the livelihood of the farmers that affects the whole economy of California is being destroyed. This is just one example of the attack on our food supply.

Much of our farmland has been destroyed by floods and severe weather conditions. Many people believe that weather is being controlled by human beings with malevolent intentions. Whether or not it is, weather has been severe and our food supply is being affected. Weather changes have always been a problem, but when human beings are meddling with it, the potential to destroy on a massive scale the food supplies of the whole world is a definite threat.

Then there is the issue of pandemics that we have been told are inevitable. Our president declared a state of emergency in our nation over the swine flu epidemic. However, some researchers after a thorough investigation of all the data from the Center for Disease Control have stated there are actually very few cases of swine flu, and that with all the media hype doctors have mistakenly diagnosed as swine flu what are actually just the usual viruses that affect people at certain times of the year. Some scientists say that this flu which combines viruses from pigs, birds and humans had to have been created in a laboratory. There are reports that the vaccine is dangerous and may cause destructive diseases later in life.

There is so much we could say here about polluted water, polluted air, radiation exposure, chemical and biological warfare and other destructive elements in our environment that can cause sickness and death. Truly there are many destructive forces coming against us, but our God is mindful of all this and he has a plan to protect his people. This next verse in our Ezekiel passage will reveal that our bodies are going to be changed so that we will not be harmed by any of these things.

Verse 12 - Crossing Over into the Promised Land
And they went every one straight forward: whither the spirit was to go, they went; and they turned not when they went.

The pronoun, "they" is referring to the subject of the previous clause in verse 11, which is bodies. "Every one" indicates there are two bodies. We know that one body is the natural body and the other body is the spiritual body. The verb, "went" tells us they are going someplace. We encountered the words "straight forward" in verse nine. "Straight" means "on the opposite side (espec. of the Jordan)," "over," "passage," "other side." "Forward" is the exact same Hebrew word as "faces," which still means "hearts."

And they went every one straight forward means:

The two bodies, the natural body and the spiritual body (they) were going (went) over to the other side of the Jordan into the Promised Land (straight) according to their heart (forward).

The next clause gives more information.

whither the spirit was to go, they went

The pronoun "they" is still referring to the bodies. This clause tells us that the bodies are going wherever the spirit leads. We have learned that in the spirit there is a human heart joined with the heart of Christ and that parables are coming forth from the imagination of these hearts. The spiritual imagination is severed from the natural imagination of the soul and is now soaring to a higher dimension. Now we see that the bodies are following the imagination in the spirit.

At this point one may ask, "How can the bodies follow where the spirit goes. Does this mean that if the person imagines being in a beautiful garden or meadow with Christ as described earlier, they disappear from the earth and literally go there?"

The answer is, "No, not yet, but that is where we are headed in the revelation of the four living creatures."

What we are seeing in the four living creatures is a PROCESS whereby human beings on earth in the end times will transition from life in this world as we have known it into the coming age of power and miracles (Heb. 6:5). We are seeing revealed in the four living creatures God's plan to perfect a human being that eventuates in the person having a glorified body such as Christ had when he appeared on earth after his resurrection. We will not have to die to receive a glorified body in these end times because our "vile body" will be changed. We will experience that which is described in Phil. 3:20,21, "For our conversation is in heaven; from whence also we look for the Saviour, the Lord Jesus Christ: who shall change our vile body, that it may be fashioned like unto his glorious body, according to the working whereby he is able even to subdue all things unto himself."

The word "conversation" means "citizenship," or "community." We are citizens in the community of heaven spiritually, but as our vile body is changed, we will enter fully into this community even though we are still on this earth. We will be like Jesus after his resurrection. He could appear or disappear yet he had flesh and bones and could eat broiled fish and honeycomb (Luke 24).

We can begin to believe more fully we are citizens in the community of heaven by using our imagination to envision ourselves there with Jesus. We can walk with him on streets of gold in the New Jerusalem. We can bathe with him in the healing river (Ezekiel 47). The more we allow our spiritual mind to focus on these higher things by forming parables in our mind, the healthier our bodies will become. Through our heart we will be entering into a higher dimension while still on earth. Our gateway into the Kingdom is in our own heart. We must guard our heart with all diligence. We must move our mind away from its usual place (Chebar) and come into a superior form of mental activity by use of parables. We must learn the language of the Kingdom.

In verse 12 of Ezekiel 1, a process has begun that will eventuate in the body putting off mortality and putting on immortality. According to 1 Cor. 15:52, we shall be changed in a moment, but the four living creatures reveal a process leading up to that instantaneous change. As this process begins, the bodies embark on a journey as they cross over Jordan into the Promised Land. The Promised Land is heaven. We will reach heaven through our heart. We are citizens of heaven even though we are on earth, but to fully believe it we must envision parables of truth in our imagination.

The last clause of this verse is:

and they turned not when they went.

The pronoun, "they," is referring to the natural body and the spiritual body.

"Turned," *cabab*, means "surround" or "border." Something that is surrounded or has a border is confined within bounds or limits. The bodies are coming out of these bounds and limitations because they "turned not" when they went.

As the process of crossing over Jordan into the Promised Land commences in the bodies, the shackles and confines of being in a human body begin to fall away. The inability to feel Christ's presence is gone and the glorious sense of his nearness is ours forever. The natural body begins to rise up into divine health. This new dimension of health will come with our participation in imagining parables. The terrible physical limitations and ill health that come with aging will fall away as we continue deepening our relationship with Christ through the parables. We will have a new understanding of healing as we learn that health flows naturally out of a relationship with Jesus as we press forward into the Promised Land and continue envisioning the parables. Sickness, aging and death have been our lot because of the sin nature inherited from Adam. In the four living creatures a process is seen whereby Jesus Christ is gradually removing the sin nature from every aspect of our being. We will see later in the four living creatures that there will come a time when all sin will be eradicated.

The following is our spiritual interpretation of verse 12:

The two bodies, the natural body and the spiritual body (they, every one) were going (went) over to the other side of the Jordan into the Promised Land (straight) according to their heart (forward). They were following wherever the spirit led them (whither the spirit was to go, they went); the bodies were leaving behind the shackles and confines of human existence (and they turned not when they went).

Parable #5

I found myself walking along the shore of the ocean. The surf splashed against my bare feet and then pulled the sand out from under them as it rushed back into the sea. The fresh scent of salt air filled my nostrils refreshing and invigorating my soul and body. I stopped for a moment to view the different shades of blue-green water stretching out before me. Suddenly I was almost knocked off my feet as a large wave unexpectedly surged against the shore soaking my rolled up pant legs almost to my waist. It was a cool evening and ordinarily the wet clothes would have sent a chill over my body, but now I only felt invigorated.

My mind gradually returned to the events of the day. It had been a good day...a very busy day filled with the typical activities of balancing ministry with family life. I felt like I had accomplished a lot and was ready for some "alone time" with God here at the beach. Although it had been a good day, one thing had troubled me. A nagging health problem that had plagued me my entire life had reared its ugly head again. The stinging, itching curse of eczema had broken out on my face, hands and arms and I had been unconsciously "digging" at it all day. The medicine that had been so effective was now priced out of my ability to afford. I had received a phone call from the pharmacist that day asking if I was sure I wanted him to fill the prescription I had dropped off that morning because it was going to cost over a thousand dollars! I immediately cancelled the order.

I forced myself to focus on the beauty around me. As the sun was descending, brilliant shades of orange, along with pink and some lavender colored the clouds...even the ocean itself was beginning to look orange. A few birds soaring out over the water, perhaps hoping for one more snack before retiring for the day, appeared to be black as they were silhouetted against the brilliant fiery sky.

I must be getting back soon, I reasoned. I don't want to be out here alone after dark. As I turned to go, I noticed something off to my right I had not seen before although I must have passed by it. In a little rocky alcove just far enough back where the waves would not reach was a fire and a lone figure of a man sitting beside it. Ordinarily I would have hastened by and ignored the man, but a deep feeling of peace and security enveloped me and something inside drew me almost irresistibly toward the lone figure and the fire much like a moth to a lamp.

The man seemed familiar to me as though I had known him for many years...perhaps an old friend. He seemed to be expecting me and motioned for me to sit near the fire across from him.

As I sat down while looking intently at the man's face, I recognized who he was. He was Jesus! He spoke saying, "You are wet from the waves and there is a chill in the air. Sit here for awhile and soon you will be warm and dry."

Indeed the fire was already warming my cold legs. The crackling of the burning logs and the slight scent of wood smoke brought back pleasant feelings associated with family camping trips and loving fellowships of years gone by.

Jesus stirred the fire with a stick and then raised his head towards me with a look of concern emanating from his deep blue eyes. His black beard was neatly trimmed, as was his hair. To my surprise he was not dressed in a white robe as I would have expected, but rather in blue jeans and a khaki shirt. Everything about him was very masculine with a strength about him that gave me a sense of well-being and a knowing that no evil could befall me when I was in his presence.

As though reading my mind he said, "You need never fear anything because I am always with you in the same strength and loving concern you are sensing here. I have pulled the veil back for you to see and experience here tonight what is always true even when I am not visible and you have to trust me by faith."

Jesus continued, "I know of your concern over the price of the medicine. This is what will be befalling everyone in these last days. You are going to have to trust me for all your healing needs."

"But how can I do that?" I lamented. "I have tried to believe for healing many times but never could muster up enough faith."

"Yes, I know," he said. "I am going to show you tonight how to find a deeper relationship with me whereby I can heal your body of everything if you are willing to spend the time with me. Let's start healing that eczema tonight."

"I'm all for that!" I exclaimed.

"I want my people to be healed," Jesus continued, "but even more than that, I want them to love me and desire to be with me.

Only then will I be able to bring them into the dimension of spirituality and wholeness I have for my church of the end times."

Jesus moved over closer to me and indicated he wanted me to lie on the sand with my head in his lap. "I long to be close to my people," he said, "but many keep me at arms' length. They don't understand that my holiness does not mean I am untouchable. I shed my blood for each of you so that we could have a close relationship. Would a loving father never stroke his child's head? Would a bridegroom never touch his bride?"

"No," I responded.

Jesus continued, "Close our eyes and rest here with your head in my lap. Listen to the sound of the waves splashing up on the shore. Hear the crackling of the warm fire. Breathe deeply and relax."

I did as he instructed. I could feel the tension leaving my muscles. The itching of my skin subsided. For the first time in days I felt truly relaxed and at peace.

Jesus said, "I asked you to focus on these sounds because I want you to remember them and be able to recall them at any time. When the stress and concerns of your life begin to nag at you, draw apart with me and let your mind come back to this place. See the beauty you have seen tonight in your mind. Recall the sounds of the waves, the fire, and my voice. I will always be here waiting for you. You can come here any time you choose.

I opened my eyes to see Jesus reaching into his shirt pocket. He pulled out a small, golden vial that had been engraved with filigree. He removed the lid, poured some fragrant oil into his hands and began to gently massage the oil into my face. Ever so gently his fingers glided over my eyelids...one of my worst places for eczema. His movements were rhythmic, slow and incredibly gentle. The oil was warm and I could feel it penetrating my skin as the fragrance filled my nose with a scent sweeter than the freshest flower.

Jesus continued to instruct me. "As you lie here with your eyes closed, I want you to picture what you are seeing here tonight in your mind. Envision my nail-scarred hands gently massaging the warm, healing balm into your skin so that after you leave this place tonight, you will be able to return here in your mind at any time. The more you return to this experience in your mind, the stronger it will become until you will actually feel my hands touching your face.

"I want you to think about what my Word says about healing when you meet with me here. Thank me for healing you and don't allow the enemy to put his lies in your mind. As you come here often to be with me, over a period of time you will find the problem with eczema will disappear."

Jesus continued gently massaging the oil into each area of my skin plagued with the insistent rash. We were quiet for a time as I lay there totally relaxed, concentrating on his gentle touch and the sounds and scents of the experience. Never had I known such peace.

Then Jesus said, "Your healing will take time because I am healing you from the inside out. You need to change some of your thinking to be totally free of the eczema. Have you ever wondered why the rash is on certain parts of your body and not on others?"

"Yes," I have thought about that," I replied.

Jesus continued, "Think about your feelings about yourself connected with aging."

I knew right where he was headed with this. "I have hated the wrinkles and effects of aging apparent on my face and arms, the very places where I am troubled with the rash," I responded.

"Yes," he said, "and what you are doing is rejecting those parts of your body. When you reject any part of yourself, you are opening the door to the enemy."

"Oh, Lord, please forgive me!" I exclaimed. "I know this is a part of my self-love that still exists and needs to go. I repent of agreeing with what the world says about a woman's appearance rather than what your Word says. I know you find beauty in a quiet, gentle spirit. The most important beauty is what is inside, not what is temporal and on the outside."

"You will overcome this," Jesus promised. "If you will be faithful to spend time with me here and focus the eyes of your heart on me, your self-love will go. You have died a lot to what others think of you. This part will go quickly as you allow me to tell you how beautiful I think you are."

Then he asked, "Do you feel weak or sick in your body as you age?"

"No, Lord. Because of your activity in my life, I feel healthier and stronger than I have ever been."

"Then focus on that and where you are headed as you draw close to me. You know from your studies that I am doing a work that will culminate in the total removal of all carnality and its effects from your soul and body, but first all your thinking must align itself with mine. It will help if you visualize yourself as I see you...in total perfection.

"All this seems so impossible," I said.

Jesus answered, "Just remember that with man it is impossible, but with me, all things are possible. It is time, my Beloved, to enter into the good things of the kingdom that I have prepared for those who love me. Now you must return home. It is dark. You will not see me now, but I will lead you safely home."

Verse 13 - Separating the Natural Body from the Spiritual Body

As for the likeness of the living creatures, their appearance was like burning coals of fire, and like the appearance of lamps: it went up and down among the living creatures; and the fire was bright, and out of the fire went forth lightning.

Verse 12 established that the bodies are being lifted up from the confines of human existence as they cross over Jordan into the Promised Land. Verse 13 reveals the beginning of the process necessary for this to take place.

"Likeness" is still parables.

The "living creatures" are the mature Christian persons who are having this experience of putting on immortality.

"Appearance" means "visions." These parables are in the form of visions being seen in the imagination.

"Burning coals of fire," will be interpreted according to its use in the only other place in Scripture where this phrase is seen—Leviticus 16 where we see Aaron, the high priest, entering into the Holy of Holies into the presence of God after having slain a bullock for the remission of his sins:

"And he shall take a censer full of burning coals of fire from off the altar before the LORD, and his hands full of sweet incense beaten small, and bring it within the veil: And he shall put the incense upon the fire before the LORD, that the cloud of the incense may cover the mercy seat that is upon the testimony, that he die not:"

The parables in the form of visions being envisioned by the mature Christians are taking them through the veils of their flesh into the Holy of Holies into the presence of God like the coals of fire in Lev. Notice Aaron does this "that he die not." As we participate in envisioning the parables, we too literally shall not die.

Incense spiritually refers to our prayers, praise and worship. David said in Psalms 141, "Let my prayer be set forth before thee as incense." (See also Luke 1:8-10, Rev. 5:8; 8:3.) We will find that prayer, praise and worship take on a whole new dimension through the envisioning of parables. The parables will transition us beyond mere words into experience and presence.

Our spiritual interpretation for verse 13 thus far reads:

As for the parables (as for the likeness) coming forth from the mature Christians in the end times (of the living creatures), these visions (their appearance) were taking these people through the veils of their flesh into the presence of God that they would not die (was like burning coals of fire) as prayer, praise and worship went beyond mere words causing them to experience God's presence in a new dimension.

If these people are not going to die, something must be done to change the mortal body so death can no longer work in its members. Death came upon all humankind through Adam and Eve's disobedience. When they lived in the garden before they sinned, there was no sickness and no death. God warned them that if they disobeyed him by eating from the tree of the knowledge of good and evil, they would die on that day. God was true to his word and cast them out of the garden which began the process of death in them. Death did not fully manifest until they had lived a few hundred years. The Bible says that with God a day is as a thousand years and a thousand years is as a day. No one ever lived a thousand years after sin entered into humanity by Adam and Eve's sin.

There can be no doubt that death is directly related to the sin nature we all inherited by virtue of being human beings. This in no way means that people who have a lot of sickness are more sinful than people who are not sick. However, it does mean that if the sin nature that is resident in our natural bodies because of our humanity were to be removed, we would no longer suffer sickness or death. If we are living in the end times and going through the experience revealed by the four living creatures, we should expect to become healthier and stronger even as we age. The removal of the sin nature is a gradual process and we participate in it at God's direction through our obedience to him and the work of the parables.

In verse 11 we learned we have a spiritual body. In verse 12 we were told that the physical body and the spiritual body are leaving the confines and shackles of human existence as they follow the leading of the spirit. Next we will see the process we will go through as our mortal body is changed into a glorified body.

This next clause will reveal that the first step in our physical transformation is the separation of the natural body from the spiritual body:

and like the appearance of lamps: it went up and down among the living creatures;

The word "like" is not in the original Hebrew text.

"Appearance" continues to mean "visions."

"Among," *beyn*, means "asunder," meaning to separate into parts or pieces.

There are two Hebrew words for "lamps" in the Old Testament. The word used here, *lappiyd*, is a "firebrand," or a "burning torch," a more powerful word than the other word for lamp, *niyr*, meaning "to glisten," "a candle," or "lamp." To gain an understanding of *lappiyd* in this Ezekiel passage, we must examine how it is used elsewhere in Scripture.

Samson

Lappiyd is the word used in Judges 15 where Samson "put a firebrand in the midst between two tails" of the foxes. The firebrand or lamp went between the two bodies of the foxes dividing them. We have been learning about the fact that we have two bodies—a physical body and a spiritual body. When Ezekiel says, like the appearance of lamps: it went up and down among the living creatures, "among" means "between." In a vision (appearance) the lamp went up and down between the living creatures separating the physical body from the spiritual body.

"And Samson said concerning them, now shall I be more blameless than the Philistines, though I do them a displeasure. And Samson went and caught three hundred foxes, and took firebrands, and turned tail to tail, and put a firebrand in the midst between two tails. And when he had set the brands on fire, he let them go into the standing corn of the Philistines, and burnt up both the shocks, and also the standing corn, with the vineyards and olives."

Samson was driving the enemy out of the land. The land is our body. Our enemy, the Philistines, has robbed us of our health and caused us to grow old and die. When the firebrands between the foxes went forth, they burned up all the sustenance of the enemy. There was nothing left for the enemy to feed upon. When the sin nature is removed from our body, there will be nothing for the enemy, Satan, to feed upon. He will have no place in our body because there will be nothing to sustain him. God will have burned away all the sin nature.

There were three hundred foxes. Three hundred is the number of divine deliverance. Bullinger says nothing about this number, but we know it means divine deliverance because of the way it is consistently used throughout Scripture. We see it in the book of Judges where Gideon and his three hundred men defeated the Midianites. It is seen in 2 Sam. 23:18, "And Abishai, the brother of Joab, the son of Zeruiah, was chief among three. And he lifted up his spear against three hundred, and slew them, and had the name among three." A similar account is in 1 Chron. 11:11 "...Jashobeam, an Hachmonite, the chief of the captains: he lifted up his spear against three hundred slain by him at one time." Obviously these were miraculous accounts of God's divine intervention in bringing deliverance to his people.

In 2 Chron. 9:16 concerning Solomon we read, "And three hundred shields made he of beaten gold: three hundred shekels of gold went to one shield." Gold represents the pure divine nature of the Lord Jesus Christ. When all sin is removed from every aspect of our being, we will have complete divine deliverance and have the character of Christ with no mixture of our own sin nature. We will be pure gold.

Notice what Samson said before he tied the firebrands between the foxes' tails. He said, "Now shall I be more blameless than the Philistines." As the lamp or firebrand of the Lord passes between our parts (between the physical body and the spiritual body) we will be in a process of becoming blameless also. We will be delivered of the sin nature that causes us to become sick and old and eventually die. We will have divine deliverance. First God will separate the spiritual body from the physical body. Then he will remove the sin nature from the physical body and we shall be changed (*allasso* – to make different [1 Cor. 15:51]).

Gideon

In the story of Gideon in Judges, we see the number 300 again combined with *lappiyd* (lamps). Gideon had three companies each comprised of 100 men. "And the three companies blew the trumpets, and brake the pitchers, and held the lamps in their left hands, and the trumpets in their right hands to blow withal: and they cried, The sword of the LORD, and of Gideon."

We have learned that our right side is the spirit side of our being and the left side is our soul. The trumpet here represents the voice of the Lord. "I was in the Spirit on the Lord's day, and heard behind me a great voice, as of a trumpet saying, I am Alpha and Omega, the first and the last..." (Rev. 1:10,11a).

We have learned that parables are the word of the Lord coming forth from the heart of Christ joined with our heart in the spirit on the right side of our being. The parables are proclaiming the truth of the Lord like a trumpet.

The concordance shows us that the word "trumpet" has something to do with "incising" or "cutting." The blast of a trumpet incises the airwaves. It splits the air with its piercing sound. The trumpet in the right hand is a type of the parables as the word of God coming forth from the spirit. The trumpet pierces through the air. It incises the air. The word "spirit" also means "air." The word of the Lord (trumpet) is cutting away the spiritual side (incising the air) from the natural side.

Gideon's men did not have a sword. They only had pitchers with lamps and trumpets, yet they cried out, "The sword of the Lord, and of Gideon."

We read about the sword of the Lord in Heb. 4:12, "For the word of God is quick, and powerful, and sharper than any twoedged sword, piercing even to the dividing asunder of soul and spirit, and of the joints and marrow, and is a discerner of the thoughts and intents of the heart." In this account of Gideon we see a picture of the word of the Lord separating the joints from the marrow.

The joints speak of the natural body. Joints are places of weakness in that they can become diseased with arthritis or worn down with age. Also they can get out of joint when subjected to a forceful blow. Ahab died when he was struck in the joints of his harness (1 Kings 22:34). The hollow of Jacob's thigh was out of joint after God touched him there (Gen. 32:25). Death by crucifixion caused the bones to be out of joint (Ps. 22:14). When Belshazzar saw the fingers of a man's hand writing on the wall, his "countenance was changed, and his thoughts troubled him so that the joints of his loins were loosed, and his knees smote against one another" (Dan. 5:6). Clearly joints are associated with weakness and death—two inevitabilities of the natural body.

Marrow, on the other hand, speaks of eternal life. Blood is produced in the bone marrow, and it is because of the shed blood of Jesus Christ that we have eternal life. Marrow in Scripture is always associated with health and blessing (Job 21:14; Ps. 63:5; Prov. 3:8; Isa. 25:6).

In these end times as God prepares us to enter into immortality, he will not only be separating the soul from the spirit, but also the natural body from the spiritual body and removing weakness from the natural body.

Continuing with the account of Gideon and his men, we see they had pitchers in their left hands. These pitchers are containers made of clay. Therefore, a pitcher is an earthen vessel. As we look to the New Testament we will gain a clearer understanding of what these pitchers signify.

Paul states,

> ...we have this treasure in earthen vessels, that the excellency of the power may be of God, and not of us." And also, "...we know that if our earthly house of this tabernacle were dissolved, we have a building of God, an house not made with hands, eternal in the heavens. For in this we groan, earnestly desiring to be clothed upon with our house which is from heaven: if so be that being clothed we shall not be found naked. For we that are in this tabernacle do groan, being burdened: not for that we would be unclothed, but clothed upon, that mortality might be swallowed up of life. Now he that hath wrought us for the selfsame thing is God, who also hath given unto us the earnest of the Spirit (2 Cor. 4:6 – 5:5).

Here in 2 Corinthians Paul speaks of our body as being an earthen vessel in which death works as our outward man perishes. It is our earthly house that will pass away. We have another body (our house which is from heaven) which is our spiritual body that we live in after death. However, when this mortal puts on immortality, the two bodies will go through a process of coming together whereby we can be on earth and be in heaven also with no death working in us.

The pitchers were in the left hand. We learned in verse ten of Ezekiel one that our left side is our natural side.

It is clear from this New Testament passage that the pitchers represent our human physical body in all its frailties. This body is an earthen vessel, our earthly house that is perishing...it is our mortal flesh. We are shown a picture of this frailty, this mortality, broken away in the Gideon passage where the pitchers are broken and the light shines forth. Hidden in this Old Testament type is a picture of human beings in the end times putting off mortality and putting on immortality.

Having established that the spiritual body is being separated from the physical body as the frailties of our humanity are broken away, let us take another look at this verse in Judges.

"And the three companies blew the trumpets, and brake the pitchers, and held the lamps in their left hands, and the trumpets in their right hands to blow withal: and they cried, The sword of the LORD, and of Gideon."

The number "three" means "divine completeness or perfection" (Bullinger).

"Companies," according to Strong's Concordance, means "the highest part."

"Blew," *taqa'*, means "smite." "To smite," according to Webster, is to "bring into a specified condition by a blow."

The word for lamp, *lappiyd*, is likened to salvation in Isa. 62:1,2, "For Zion's sake will I not hold my peace, and for Jerusalem's sake I will not rest, until the righteousness thereof go forth as brightness, and the salvation thereof as a lamp that burneth. And the Gentiles shall see thy righteousness, and all kings thy glory: and thou shalt be called by a new name, which the mouth of the LORD shall name." A few verses down in this passage we read, "...as the bridegroom rejoiceth over the bride, so shall thy God rejoice over thee." This passage is speaking about coming into the completion of the Lord Jesus Christ free from the sin nature. Then the glory of God and his righteousness will be evident in us. We will be married to Christ and have a new name.

The name, Gideon, means "he that breaks," and "destroyer."

Putting together all of the above, we find the following spiritual interpretation of this verse in Judges:

In order to come into divine perfection and completeness (three), the highest part of our being which is our spirit (companies) must sound forth the word of the Lord in the language of parables seen as visions (blow the trumpets). These trumpet sounds, or the parables, are incisive in that they sever the spiritual part of our being from the natural part. Our physical body that is of the earth and therefore subject to death will have the mortality broken away (and brake the pitchers). We will then be able to seize hold of full salvation (held the lamps in their left hands). The word of the Lord (trumpets) sounding forth from our spirit (in their right hands) brings our physical body into the specified condition determined by God (blow). This is all done by the word of the Lord as it destroys all mortality from our being (the sword of the Lord and of Gideon).

Abraham

This same word for "lamps," *lappiyd*, is seen again in the Old Testament as a lamp that passes between animal parts. In Genesis 15, "...the word of the Lord came unto Abram in a vision." (Remember, the parables coming forth from the spirit are the word of the Lord in the form of a vision.) God showed him the stars in the heavens and said, "So shall thy seed be." We may have thought of this illustration in terms of numbers only, but it is easy to see that we are also to be in the POSITION of the stars in the heavens. When we receive our inheritance of a glorified body free from all sickness, aging and death, we will shine forth as the stars in the heavens as prophesied in Dan. 12:3, "And they that be wise shall shine as the brightness of the firmament; and they that turn many to righteousness as the stars for ever and ever."

Abram asked God, "How shall I know that I shall inherit it?" Then the Scriptures again show us a picture of the process of coming into perfection in the end times. Abram took the bodies of three different animals, each three years of age, and divided them in the middle at the word of the Lord. These would represent the physical body being divided—those parts that become part of the glorified body separated from the parts of mortality to be destroyed. Then he took two birds, a turtledove and a young pigeon, but these he did not divide (higher bodies meaning spiritual bodies). "And it came to pass, that, when the sun went down, and it was dark, behold a smoking furnace, and a burning lamp that passed between those pieces."

We are living in the end of the age (when the sun went down). There is great darkness of terrible evil coming upon the earth (and it was dark). God is separating the parts of our bodies, the sin from the natural body and the natural body from the spiritual body, by the smoking furnace that burns out all sin nature and the burning lamp (*lappiyd*) of full salvation that pass between the parts. We are the descendants of Abram that are entering in to possess the land. The birds that were not cut in half represent the spiritual (heavenly) body because birds fly in the heavenly realm. The spiritual body will be separated from the physical body but the spiritual body itself will not have to be divided.

My Experience

I was able to feel the Lord separating my two bodies almost immediately after my spiritual body was awakened. We have learned that our right side is our spiritual side and the left side is our natural side. I could feel myself being divided in the middle. It was a constant tingling feeling that moved up and down the very center of my body. There was absolutely no pain…just a strong feeling of God's presence at work. It took several days…I don't remember exactly how many, but it was very pleasant. When this happens to you, you will know what God is doing.

I believe that very soon something extremely frightening will take place worldwide that will strike terror in the hearts of all people. At that time, I believe many true Christians will feel their spiritual body being awakened. This will be a sign to them that Jesus is very close and is lifting them up to a higher realm in him. This will be very comforting for them at this time of terror. Immediately after their spiritual body is awakened, they should feel the two bodies being separated.

It would be beneficial to check one more place in Scripture where *lappiyd* is used. Daniel had a vision of the Lord where his eyes were described as "lamps of fire" (Dan. 10:6).

When envisioning parables in my mind, the Lord has encouraged me to look into his eyes and see his love and compassion for me. It takes time to develop a picture of the Lord's face in one's mind and even more time to imagine his eyes. Once this ability has been developed, it is an incredible experience to look into his eyes. It reminds me of the words of a song:

Turn your eyes upon Jesus
Look full in his wonderful face
And the things of earth will grow strangely dim
In the light of his glory and grace.

This little song describes exactly what happens as we repeatedly practice looking into the Lord's eyes. We feel his presence and things of this earth lose their grip on us because we are focusing the eyes of our heart on Christ thereby bringing earthly things into their proper perspective. The eyes of the Lord are like a lamp, burning the sin nature out of us.

Before examining the rest of verse 13, we will summarize this clause, *like the appearance of lamps: it went up and down among the living creatures*:

> *These parables in the form of visions (and like the appearance) were the word of the Lord coming forth from the spirit. The word of the Lord was like a sharp two-edged sword separating the spiritual body from the natural body while removing human frailty and mortality from the natural body (of lamps: it went up and down among the living creatures).*

Removing Sin Nature from the Natural Body
    The last clause of verse 13 states, *and the fire was bright,*

The fire is the presence of God. Our God is a consuming fire and he has come to cleanse us from all the sin nature in our body. God works from the inside out in that he begins in our spirit, works in our soul and then in our body. As Paul explains in Romans, we have a body of sin.

"Knowing this, that our old man is crucified with him, that the body of sin might be destroyed, that henceforth we should not serve sin" (Rom. 6:6). (It is interesting that Romans is the sixth book of the New Testament so Rom. 6:6 is like 666—the number of the Antichrist. Everything in us that is anti-Christ must be destroyed.)

In verse 12 of Romans 6, we are warned, "Let not sin therefore reign in your mortal body, that ye should obey it in the lusts thereof." In the four living creatures, God is removing the sin that has been in our bodies as a result of the fall. When all the sin is removed from our bodies, we will no longer have to contend with the lusts of the flesh. Our bodies will come into perfect agreement with the word of God.

The word "bright," is the same as "brightness" that we encountered in verse four of Ezekiel 1. Webster informs us that "brightness" means "the luminous aspect of a color (as distinct from its hue) by which it is regarded as approaching the maximum luminance of pure white."

Jesus Christ is the maximum luminance of pure white. The presence of God is judging us here in our body according to that standard and we are required to cooperate with him in this endeavor by envisioning the parables.

The clause, and the fire was bright, is interpreted as:

The presence of God was burning up the sin nature in the natural bodies of these mature Christians (and the fire) and their bodies were being judged according to the standard of the perfect body of the Lord Jesus Christ (was bright).

Continuing with the final clause of this verse, *and out of the fire went forth lightning:*

The Hebrew word for "went forth" is *yatsa'*. *Yatsa'* has many definitions among which are "be condemned" and "be risen." As the eyes of God are moving between the natural and spiritual bodies and separating sin from the natural body, all the sin nature in us is condemned and all that is not sin in us rises up into God's presence.

There are four different Hebrew words for lightning in the Old Testament. This particular word, *baraq*, is most often associated with God's presence and judgment. It is seen in Exodus 19 where thunder and lightning flashed forth from Mt. Sinai.

Baraq is used in 2 Sam. 22: "The LORD thundered from heaven, and the most High uttered his voice. And he sent out arrows, and scattered them; lightning, and discomfited them."

Verses similar to the above are seen in Psalms 18, 77 and 97.

In Job 20:25 *baraq* is translated "glittering sword." Knowing that the Holy Spirit could have used other words for "lightning," it is significant that he used one that can be translated "glittering sword" because we are seeing in this Ezekiel passage the separation of natural and spiritual bodies and the cutting away of sin from the natural body that can only be done according to Heb. 4:12, "For the word of God is quick, and powerful, and sharper than any twoedged sword, piercing even to the dividing asunder of soul and spirit, and of the joints and marrow, and is a discerner of the thoughts and intents of the heart."

This separation of the natural side of our being from the spiritual side is a gradual process. Each verse of the four living creatures gives us more insights into how this process progresses. We see here in this verse that God is judging us according to the standard of His Son Jesus. God reveals to us where we fall short, we repent and God removes more of our sin nature. As the sin nature is removed, our natural bodies become healthier and stronger. In this way our body is crossing over Jordan into a new land of health and stamina.

Our last clause may be interpreted as:

And as a result of this judging (out of the fire), the sin nature was being condemned and all that was not sin was being raised up into the presence of God (went forth) as the natural body and spiritual body were being divided by a glittering sword which was the Word of God [Heb. 4:12] (lightning).

The following is our spiritual interpretation of verse 13 in its entirety:

As for the parables (as for the likeness) coming forth from the mature Christians in the end times (of the living creatures), these visions (their appearance) were taking these people through the veils into the presence of God that they would not die (was like burning coals of fire) as prayer, praise and worship went beyond mere words causing them to experience God's presence in a new dimension. These parables in the form of visions (and like the appearance) were the word of the Lord coming forth from the spirit. The word of the Lord was like a sharp two-edged sword separating the spiritual body from the natural body while removing human frailty and mortality from the natural body (of lamps: it went up and down among the living creatures).The presence of God was burning up the sin nature in these people (and the fire) and was judging them according to the standard of the Lord Jesus Christ (was bright), and as a result of this judging (out of the fire), the sin nature was being condemned and the good was being raised up into the presence of God (went forth) as the natural body and the spiritual body were being divided by a glittering sword which was the Word of God [Heb.4:12] (lightning).

It is imperative we remember that we see according to what is in our heart. The more we purify our heart, the more clearly we will be able to see Jesus and heavenly things. Jesus said, "The light of the body is the eye: if therefore thine eye be single, thy whole body shall be full of light. But if thine eye be evil, thy whole body shall be full of darkness. If therefore the light that is in thee be darkness, how great is that darkness!" (Matt. 6:22, 23).

This is talking about seeing through our heart. The human eye is physically an organ of the body that is neither good nor evil. How we perceive what that eye sees is directly correlated to what is in our heart. Our heart can be clouded with jealousy, unforgiveness, bitter root judgments, inner vows and such things that render us incapable of seeing things as they truly are. Let me give an example.

When we were pastoring a church in Ohio, a woman made an appointment to see me. Her reason for coming was to tell me how deeply I had hurt her by my "disapproval" of her involvement in sports. I had no idea what she was talking about. Why would I care whether or not this woman played sports? I was mystified. Then I sensed the Lord's wisdom and asked her, "Did your mother disapprove of your participation in sports?" She answered in the affirmative. That was the crux of the whole problem. She perceived me to be a mother figure. Since her mother disapproved of her sports activities she assumed I did too. Her eye was not single. She didn't see me for who I was, she saw me with her mother superimposed over me, so to speak. I led her in prayer to forgive her mother and to break the judgment she had made against her...a judgment that clouded her ability to see other women for who they are.

We are like this as we try to envision Jesus. Some women who have been abused are afraid to visualize Jesus because they have been so abused by men. Their heart contains the belief that all men are abusers. It will take time and a lot of prayer and forgiveness to come to the place that they can see men according to each one's character rather than lumping them all together as abusers.

Whatever we believe about ourselves, others and our experiences in life will determine how we see our self as well as how we see Jesus. Some people see their self as being so inferior they could not conceive of the idea of being near Jesus. It takes some spiritual maturity to have a heart clear enough to begin to see Jesus and envision heavenly things.

As we concentrate on heavenly things we will become like that upon which we set our focus. The more we think about "whatsoever things are true, whatsoever things are honest, whatsoever things are just, whatsoever things are pure, whatsoever things are lovely, whatsoever things are of good report," the more we will become like these things. "If there be any virtue, if there be any praise, think on these things" (Phil. 4:8).

The more we allow ourselves to die to the things of this world, the more we will be able to see Jesus as we focus our imagination on the parables and envision heavenly things. The Holy Spirit will be cooperating with us, identifying and burning up the sin nature and filling us with more of Christ.

As we labor to enter into new levels of holiness, the enemy is working overtime to fill our minds with sorcery, immorality and violence through our television programs and movies. Even most programming with "G" ratings portrays rebellious attitudes, revenge, trickery or evil supernatural phenomena. We must guard our hearts with all diligence.

"Beloved, now are we the sons of God, and it doth not yet appear what we shall be: but we know that, when he shall appear, we shall be like him; for we shall see him as he is. And every man that hath this hope in him purifieth himself, even as he is pure" (1 John 3:2, 3). The only way we are going to see Jesus appear is if we become like him because we can only see spiritually according to what is in our own heart. Nothing but our own carnality stands between us and a full revelation of Jesus Christ.

Practical Suggestions for Forming Parables

Here are some suggestions that may help in learning to form parables in your mind. First of all, you will need a regular quiet time each day to work on them which may require eliminating some other things from your schedule. It helps to have a set time and a certain place where you do this so you will feel comfortable and be more likely to maintain constancy in this new discipline. Once you have learned to form the parables you will be able to think of them wherever you are, but you still need the quiet time away from distractions to really concentrate on your relationship with the Lord.

One of the first things you need to do is learn to picture Jesus. I found this difficult and even impossible to do on my own. I decided to find some artist's picture of Jesus that I really liked and use that to help spark my own imagination. I chose the paintings of Jesus by the artist Richard Hook. These pictures depict Jesus as strong and masculine. There are so many paintings of Jesus, particularly from the Renaissance period, that make him look weak and unattractive. It is true that the Bible says he was not desirable to look upon. "…he hath no form nor comeliness; and when we shall see him, there is no beauty that we should desire him" (Isa. 53:2). However, we need to remember that this described him before his death and resurrection. He now has a glorified, resurrected body that is absolutely perfect.

I believe his appearance can be whatever we want it to be. This is why there is no description of him in the Bible. People were not able to recognize him after his resurrection except when he opened their eyes. Mary in the garden thought he was the gardener at first. The men on the road to Emmaus did not recognize him until he broke bread with them at dinner. So with this in mind, I think we can feel free to choose any picture of him in our mind that appeals to us personally.

Next we need a setting for our parables. We want some of our parables to be about heaven and some about earth. For the heavenly ones, we need to determine what we think heaven looks like. The Lord will lead us in this. I believe there must be vast dimensions of heaven most of which I could not comprehend. However, according to some dreams I've had, I do think there may be a part of it that is like earth only absolutely perfect. This is what I visualize.

I have several places in my mind that have been established over many years of visualizing. Some of them are from my childhood where I was surrounded by the beauty of the Rocky Mountains of Colorado. Other places are by the ocean. My family moved to Maryland in my later teen years where we lived on the Chesapeake Bay. I have pleasant memories of evenings on the beach with the fragrance of honeysuckle in the air. These have formed the foundation for some of the parables I envision.

It also helps to find beautiful pictures to commit to memory. I especially like some of the pictures by Thomas Kinkade, "the painter of light." His garden scenes have helped me, but my favorite one is a picture of a small village nestled at the base of high mountain peaks. A little stream flows down from the mountains and through the village. There is an arched bridge over the stream with a rowboat underneath resting against a bank that is covered with flowering bushes of red, orange, purple and white. On one side of the stream is a church. There are houses on both sides of the little creek with flowering trees and gardens everywhere.

Once I committed this picture to memory, I was able to go there with Jesus and interact with him in this beautiful setting. We can stand together on the bridge, lean on the railing and look down at the fish swimming in the water below. We can get in the rowboat and float downstream together. We have climbed up the mountain trail to an old gold mine up near the top of the mountain. We went inside and explored. Along the way, we see things and Jesus teaches me. Once I formed this place inside and repeatedly went there, the Holy Spirit helped guide me into many inspired experiences with Jesus. Some of my visions have been based on particular passages of scripture, but others have not. The most important thing about the vision/parables is that they be relational. We want to visualize interaction with Jesus using what we know from the scriptures of his character and personality.

Some of our parables need to be about our life on earth. In these I imagine Jesus with me wherever I am. He is with me in the car, walking along the road or through the woods, working around my house...wherever I go I try to remember to imagine Jesus with me. I find it more difficult to imagine this because I am distracted with all the activity around me. The heavenly visions I focus on when I am alone are much easier for me, but the more I concentrate on Jesus with me wherever I go, the easier it becomes.

Chapter Nine
Being Conformed to the Image of Christ

Verse 14 - Experiencing God's Presence and Love
And the living creatures ran and returned as the
appearance of a flash of lightning.

The Hebrew word for "flash" means "to lighten." The word
"lighten" reminds me of 2 Cor. 4:6, "For God who commanded
the light to shine out of darkness, hath shined in our hearts, to
give the light of the knowledge of the glory of God in the face of
Jesus Christ."

Is this not what is taking place here in Ezekiel? As we focus
on seeing Christ in our imagination, the light of God shines into
our heart and we receive and experience the knowledge and
glory of God. Remember in verse 12 we learned that our natural
and spiritual bodies are crossing over into the Promised Land. In
verse 13 our natural and spiritual bodies were separated. In this
new dimension, when we focus our imagination to envision the
face of Christ, we feel his presence. To feel his presence is to
feel his love because he is love.

Paul prayed in Ephesians 3 that, "Christ may dwell in your
hearts by faith; that ye, being rooted and grounded in love, may
be able to comprehend with all saints what is the breadth, and
length, and depth, and height; and to know the love of Christ,
which passeth knowledge, that ye might be filled with all the
fullness of God." Only as we experience the love of God will we
come into his fullness.

Paul prayed in Ephesians 3 that, "Christ may dwell in your
hearts by faith; that ye, being rooted and grounded in love, may
be able to comprehend with all saints what is the breadth, and
length, and depth, and height; and to know the love of Christ,
which passeth knowledge, that ye might be filled with all the
fullness of God." Only as we experience the love of God will we
come into his fullness. In these end times we will physically and

emotionally feel his love in a new dimension as we choose to enter into his presence via our imagination.

Lightning in the New Testament is associated with the second coming of Christ, "For as the lightning cometh out of the east, and shineth even unto the west; so shall also the coming of the Son of man be" (Matt. 24:27). The Encyclopedia Britannica says lightning is formed when a cloud with negative charges induces a corresponding positive charge on the earth's surface. As the leader (negative charge) approaches the ground, the fields between the charges increase so that a positive upward leader develops from the earth. Over open terrain, the two leaders unite a few meters above the ground. Following this union, a massive surge of current moves up the channel at very great velocity. The result is a spectacular return stroke.

I would like to examine this again and insert some of my observations about how the second coming of Christ could correlate to lightning striking the earth. The cloud with negative charges (Christ coming in the clouds [Matt. 4:30]) induces (calls me) a corresponding (to be like him) positive charge (the positive and negative charges seek each other out to be completed as a bride and groom seek each other in order to be united in marriage) on the earth's surface (in my soul—earth as the soul will be explained in the next verse of Ezekiel 1).

The two leaders unite a few meters above ground (Then we which are alive and remain shall be caught up together with them in the clouds, to meet the Lord in the air [1 Thes. 4:17]). Following this union (marriage to Christ), a massive surge of current moves up the channel at very great velocity (In a moment, in the twinkling of an eye, at the last trump: for the trumpet shall sound, and the dead shall be raised incorruptible, and we shall be changed. For this corruptible must put on incorruption, and this mortal must put on immortality. So when this corruptible shall have put on incorruption, and this mortal shall have put on immortality, then shall be brought to pass the saying that is written, "Death is swallowed up in victory" [1 Cor. 15:52-54]). When we are caught up in the clouds to meet the Lord in the air, we are not talking about rising several thousand feet off the earth into literal clouds of water vapor. This is all taking place in a spiritual dimension right here on earth.

And continuing on with the Encyclopedia Britannica explanation of lightning...the result is a spectacular return stroke (so shall we ever be with the Lord). We are raised up to be with him but the instant we are united with him, we are filled with power and return to earth like a flash of lightning.

I believe we will see this is what is happening here in the living creatures; however, this is not a one time only experience. Let's take another look at verse 14:

And the living creatures ran and returned as the appearance of a flash of lightning.

The Hebrew word for "ran," *ratsa'*, also means "to delight in." The word for "returned," *shuwb*, means "to retreat," and "often."

Using our above definitions, our spiritual interpretation for verse 14 is:

The mature Christians (the living creatures) delighted in (ran) experiencing the parables in the form of visions that were drawing them into the presence of God and removing the sin nature from their lives (previous verse). They retreated often in their imagination to experience God's presence and feel his love (and returned). These visions (as the appearance) were causing the light of the knowledge of the glory of God in the face of Jesus Christ to shine in their hearts. Different aspects of their being were rising to meet the Lord in the air where they were uniting with him and then returning in glorious power as they were putting off mortality and putting on immortality (flash of lightning).

This is happening little by little, or from glory to glory, as we continually return in our imagination to envision the parables. Different aspects of our carnality are separated and burned away in the judging fire of God as the good that is left rises to be with the Lord one aspect at a time.

We see this explained in 2 Cor. 3:15-18, "But even unto this day, when Moses is read, the veil is upon their heart. Nevertheless when it shall turn to the Lord, the veil shall be taken away. Now the Lord is that Spirit: and where the Spirit of the Lord is, there is liberty. But we all, with open face beholding as in a glass the glory of the Lord, are changed into the same image from glory to glory, even as by the Spirit of the Lord."

We all have veils of carnality over our heart that block our vision of Jesus, but "when it shall turn to the Lord, the veil shall be taken away." As we draw apart in our heart in deep communion by using our imagination to envision the parables, God removes veils from our heart. We are looking as in a mirror (glass, *katoptrizomai*, means "to mirror oneself"). The more we look into the face of Christ and spend time in his presence, the more we become like Him.

My Experience

In thinking back over all my years of experiencing God's presence through the visions and parables, the one major theme throughout is God's love. Brenda's visions...there have been hundreds over the years...have all been primarily about God's love. I have had many dreams about his love too.

It is difficult for us to understand how much God loves us. We read the words in the Bible; we sing about his love and talk about it, but it is difficult to really comprehend how much he loves us. We have never known such love. We may have had glimpses through other Christians, but no human's love can possibly come close to the greatness of the love we begin to experience as we go through the experiences described here in Ezekiel.

Once the spiritual body has been awakened, we are able to feel his love in every molecule of our body. My feet feel loved. My hands and arms feel loved. This feeling of his tender love has not stopped since February 1997 when I first had this experience.

We have to know we are loved before we can love others. As we are changed into his image in these end times, the primary defining attribute we will have will be love. When we know we are truly loved, we have peace and security. Our feet are firmly planted on the Rock and nothing can shake us because we know who we are. We are his Beloved. We are the apple of his eye. We share in his purpose and goals. We are one with him and we are entering his kingdom.

Verse 15 - One Wheel…Our Natural Mind
Now as I beheld the living creatures, behold one wheel upon the earth by the living creatures, with his four faces.

The first word we want to examine in this verse is "wheel." The Hebrew word for "wheel," is *'owphan*, meaning "to revolve."

Paul says to Timothy in 1 Tim. 4:15, "Meditate upon these things." This word "meditate" in Greek is *meletao* and means "to revolve in the mind," "imagine," and "meditate."

A wheel revolves. We allow something to revolve in our mind when we meditate. Putting these together we come to the conclusion that the wheel of Ezekiel 1 is the mind. We use our mind to meditate. We allow things to revolve in our mind. We go over and over something in our mind. Round and round we go in the mind as we either fret about some problem or, as in the case of the living creatures, we let parables revolve in our mind as we go over them again and again.

Thus far in Ezekiel, we have learned much about our hearts (faces) and imaginations (wings). Within our heart we have a mind. There are two different Hebrew words translated as hearts: *labe,* used widely for the feelings, the will and even the intellect; and *lêbâb*, which can also be translated "mind."

We know that we have a heart in our soul that passes one aspect at a time through the cross into our spirit. In this way the stony heart is gradually transformed into a heart of flesh in the spirit. In these mature Christians, most of the characteristics of their personality, individuality and service have passed over into the spirit. However, they still have a mind in their soul. We know this verse is speaking of the mind in the soul because it is "upon the earth."

Our understanding of "earth" will come from Andrew Juke's *Types in Genesis.* He writes that on the third day, the earth rises up out of the waters—waters, he explains as being…

> that unstable element, so quickly moved by storms, is
> the well-known type of the restless desires of the heart of
> fallen man; for "the wicked are like the troubled sea,

which cannot rest, whose waters cast up mire and dirt." Before regeneration, unquiet lusts everywhere prevail: the whole man or creature is drowned and buried in them.

On the third day the earth emerges from the waters. Up to this point the unquiet element, which is naturally uppermost in the creature, has prevailed everywhere. Light has come, and shown the waste; a heaven is formed within it; but nothing fixed or firm has yet appeared. Just as in the saint there is first light, and a heaven too within, while as yet he is all instability, with nothing firm or settled. But now the firm earth rises. The state desired by Paul, —"that we be no more tossed to and fro with every wind of doctrine, but may grow up in all things into Him who is the Head, even Christ," [Eph. 4:14,15]—here begins to be accomplished. Now the will, long buried and overwhelmed with tossing lusts, rises above them to become very fruitful; and the soul, once lost in passions, emerges from the deep, like "the earth which He hath founded for ever..."

There is yet more for us to mark in this emerging earth. Not only does it escape the floods: it comes up also into the expanse of heaven. That creature, so long buried, now mounts up to meet the skies, as though aspiring to touch and become a part of heaven, while on its swelling bosom rest the sweet waters, the clouds, which embrace and kiss the hills. When the man by resurrection is freed from restless lusts; when he comes up from under the dominion of passions into a state of rest and peace; not only is he delivered from a load, but he also meets a purer world, an atmosphere of clear and high blessing; where even his hard rocks may be furrowed into channels for the rain; heaven almost touching earth, and earth heaven...

And this is effected on the third or resurrection day; for in creation, as elsewhere, the "third day" always speaks of resurrection...

The earth rises not before the third day. Just so in the world within: much is done before this day, before we know anything of "the power of resurrection" (Phil.

3:10). But "after two days He will revive us; in the third day He will raise us up, and we shall live in His sight. Then shall we know, if we follow on to know the Lord" (Hosea 6:2,3). (Jukes 1976, 18,19)

As Jukes explains above, the earth is our soul and it rises up into resurrection life. We have seen this as a process whereby different aspects of our soul pass through the cross and enter the spirit. Before this, our soul was tossed too and fro by the pounding waves of our lustful desires. God speaks and the waters are gathered together allowing the dry land, earth, to appear. As the soul (earth) rises out of the waters one aspect at a time, it touches heaven...or as we have seen in the four living creatures, it rises into the spirit and into the presence of Jesus— the same thing as being in heaven.

Now that we have established that the "wheel" is the mind and the "earth" is the soul, let's start at the beginning of this verse and examine the remaining words in the order in which they appear.

Now as I beheld the living creatures, behold one wheel upon the earth by the living creatures, with his four faces.

The first word in the Hebrew is "beheld." The word "behold" is seen a few words later and one might assume they are the same word, but they are actually different Hebrew words. The first word, "beheld," is *ra'ah*, meaning, among other things, "discern." According to Webster, "discern" means "to separate a thing mentally from another or recognize as separate or different." The word "behold," is *hinneh*, and means "to see."

In this verse Ezekiel says he is discerning something (beheld) in these mature Christians (living creatures). He sees (behold) something is different and separate from something else (beheld). The first thing he is differentiating is in verse 15 and the second or different thing is in verse 16. As seen in the definition for discern, he is "separating a thing mentally from another thing." The things he is seeing and separating are wheels, or rather minds.

In verse 15 he sees "one" mind in the soul (earth). This word "one" could be a cardinal number denoting how many, or it could be an ordinal number indicating "order in a particular series, as the beginning or the first." For our spiritual interpretation we are seeing this as an ordinal number indicating that the wheel mentioned in this verse is the first wheel or rather the first mind. This is the mind we had before experiencing the working of the cross whereby different aspects of our heart and mind passed from the soul into the spirit.

In these mature Christians (living creatures) most of the characteristics of their personality, individuality and service have passed over into the spirit. However, they still have a mind in the heart of their soul. This is the mind that is in a heart that relates to things of the earth (with his four faces). Remember faces are hearts and the number four means, according to Bullinger, "man in his relation to the world as created." This is the mind that only understands about earthly things.

Putting together all we have learned about this verse, our spiritual interpretation is as follows:

As Ezekiel was discerning these mature Christians, he began to see something that was mental separated from something else—things that were separate and different (Now as I beheld the living creatures). He saw the first mind, the mind of the soul in these mature Christians (behold one wheel upon the earth by the living creatures). This was the mind that related to things concerning the earth as created (with his four faces).

Verse 16 - The Mind of Christ in our Spiritual Mind
The appearance of the wheels and their work was like unto the colour of a beryl: and they four had one likeness: and their appearance and their work was as it were a wheel in the middle of a wheel.

In this verse he is seeing in a vision (appearance) other wheels (minds). They are separate from the above mind in that they are in the spirit. They are different because they are "like unto the colour of a beryl."

Twice in Scripture, beryl refers to the outward appearance of Christ. When Daniel sees him he exclaims, "His body also was like the beryl." In Song of Solomon "his hands are as gold rings set with beryl." To say the appearance of the wheels was like the color of beryl is to say they were like Christ. In this way they are different from the mind of the soul in verse 15. That mind could only relate to things of the earth as created. This mind is the mind of Christ. It is "a wheel in the middle of a wheel."

The New Testament tells us, "Let this mind be in you, which was also in Christ Jesus (Phil. 2:5), and "we have the mind of Christ" (1 Cor. 2:16b). In these New Testament passages we see revealed that which is concealed in the Old—the wheel within the wheel or, in other words, the mind of Christ within the mind of the individual.

Not only were the minds as the color of a beryl, but also their works were as the color of a beryl. The works that are being done by these minds in unity are obviously the works of God—miraculous works that are far beyond the ability of any human mind acting out of a human soul.

The New Testament gives more understanding of these works.

"For we are his workmanship, created in Christ Jesus unto good works, which God hath before ordained that we should walk in them" (Eph. 2:10).

"For our conversation is in heaven; from whence also we look for the Saviour, the Lord Jesus Christ: who shall change our vile body, that it may be fashioned like unto his glorious body, according to the working whereby he is able even to subdue all things unto himself" (Phil. 3:20,21).

These parables in the form of visions are coming forth from the mind of Christ joined with the mind of the person within the spirit. As these two minds work together, these visions are accomplishing the work of God within the individual, subduing all things unto the Lordship of Christ and changing their vile body into a body like his.

Before writing our spiritual interpretation of the first clause of this verse, we need to look at the word "color," *'ayin*. *'Ayin* means, among other things, "eyesight," "look" or "outward appearance." Putting together the above understandings our spiritual interpretation of the first clause is:

The visions (the appearance) coming forth from the mind of Christ within the spiritual mind of these persons (of the wheels) and the work they were doing to bring these people under the total lordship of Jesus Christ and change their vile body into a glorified body such as Jesus Christ had after his resurrection (and their work) could be seen (was like unto the colour) as being the work of Jesus Christ (of a beryl).

The next clause in verse 16 states: *and they four had one likeness.* The only words actually in the Hebrew are "four," "one" and "likeness."

"Likeness" still means "parables."

"One" means "unified," "cannot be divided," "excludes all difference, for there is no second with which it can either harmonize or conflict" (Bullinger).

"Four" means "created."

Putting these together this clause means:

These minds, the spiritual mind of the person and the mind of Christ (they), were creating (four) parables that were completely of God. There was no sin in these parables that needed to be separated out. There was nothing in these parables to conflict with the Word of God because the mind of the human being, now without sin, was in complete unity and agreement with the mind of Christ (had one likeness).

The final clause is: *and their appearance and their work was as it were a wheel in the middle of a wheel.*

"Appearance" is still "visions."

"Work" is as stated above, "We are his workmanship" (Eph. 2:10) and "...who shall change our vile body, that it may be fashioned like unto his glorious body, according to the working whereby he is able even to subdue all things unto himself" (Phil. 3:20,21).

Putting these together our spiritual interpretation of this clause is:

These parables in the form of visions (and their appearance) were the workmanship of God. They were causing all things within the persons to come under the lordship of Jesus

Christ as he was changing their vile body into a glorious body such as he had after his resurrection (and their work). All of this was coming forth from the mind of Christ within the minds of the persons (was as it were a wheel in the middle of a wheel).

Our complete spiritual interpretation of the three clauses comprising verse 16 reads as follows:

The visions (the appearance) coming forth from the mind of Christ within the spiritual mind of these persons (of the wheels) and the work they were doing to bring these people under the total lordship of Jesus Christ and change their vile body into a glorified body such as Jesus Christ had after his resurrection (and their work) could be seen (was like unto the colour) as being the work of Jesus Christ (of a beryl). These minds, the spiritual minds of the persons and the mind of Christ (they), were creating (four) parables that were completely of God. There was no sin in these parables that needed to be separated out. There was nothing in these parables to conflict with the Word of God because the mind of the human being, now without sin, was in complete unity and agreement with the mind of Christ (had one likeness). These parables in the form of visions (and their appearance) were the workmanship of God. They were causing all things within the person to come under the lordship of Jesus Christ as he was changing their vile body into a glorious body such as he had after his resurrection (and their work). All of this was coming forth from the mind of the Christ within the minds of persons (was as it were a wheel in the middle of a wheel).

A Summary Thus Far

It would seem good at this point to briefly summarize some of the major principles we have learned thus far in our Ezekiel study.

God is showing us how he is going to lift us up into his presence that we may be one with him and how he will change our vile body that it may be fashioned like unto his glorious body.

As we learned in verse one of Ezekiel 1, in order to be joined with Christ we must change our thinking. Over the years we have developed patterns of thinking that have become deeply entrenched in our minds because of our sinful responses to and limited understanding of our life experiences. These ways of thinking are contrary to the Word of God. As we progress in sanctification, we should continually be realigning our thinking with the Word of God. There will come a time when a person reaches a certain level of spiritual maturity, when the Lord will prompt them to begin using their imagination to create parables in the form of visions that are in accordance with God's Word.

At first we labor to create the parables by our own self-effort in our soul. As we continue to consistently work at forming the parables, our ability to form them will gradually pass from our self-effort in our soul to our spirit where our spiritual heart is joined with the heart of Christ.

As we continue to use our imagination to envision God's truth in story and picture form, the parables will become the very words of God because we have the mind of Christ within our mind.

Jesus taught the multitudes in parables knowing that because their hearts were hardened, they would not understand. No one will be allowed to enter the Kingdom of God with a hardened heart. Therefore, if parables can only be understood from a heart that is joined with the heart of Jesus, no one with a hardened heart can enter. This ensures that only those who are completely Christ's will be able to enter.

Parables are like another language. They are the language of the Kingdom. If we are to enter the Kingdom of God fully in these end times, we must learn this heavenly language.

Just as new languages were an important aspect of the outpouring of the Holy Spirit in Acts on the day of Pentecost, even so will this new language of parables be an essential ingredient for this last great outpouring of God's Spirit. These parables will be like the Word of God in Heb. 4:12 as they separate the soul from the spirit giving the spirit the freedom to soar to new heights with Jesus Christ free from the limitations and bondage of sin.

The parables will also be separating the natural body from the spiritual body while removing the sin nature from the natural body. The frailties of the natural body will be burned away and new health and vitality will become evident in the natural body.

The parables in the form of visions are taking the persons into the very presence of God beyond the veil releasing them into new dimensions of praise, prayer and worship as the sin nature is severed and burned up. Different aspects of their being are rising to meet the Lord in the air where they are united with him as this mortal is putting on immortality. The fact that the Scriptures say we must "put on" immortality implies that we have our part in this transforming process. We are seeing here that our interaction in forming parables is one way of participating in this process.

The persons going through this process have the mind of Christ within their own spiritual mind leading them in the formation of the parables in the form of visions. These visions are causing all aspects of their being to come under the lordship of Jesus Christ. The visions are also God's workmanship changing their vile body into a body like unto his glorious body.

Chapter Ten
Coming into Agreement with the Word of God

Verse 17- The Physical Body Agrees with the Word
When they went, they went upon their four sides: and they turned not when they went.

This verse shows how the visions will cause every part of us, even our physical body, to come into agreement with the Word of God.

In this verse we encounter a new word "sides." "Sides," *reba'* in Hebrew, may also be translated "square." According to Webster, "square" means "to test or adjust with regard to straightness or evenness (to square a surface with a straight edge); to settle, adjust, make right (as to square an account); to make equal (to square the score of a game); to bring into agreement, make to conform, to bring into correct position with regard to a line, course, etc."

The above definition of "square" (keeping in mind "sides," *reba'* also means "square") tells us exactly the work that is being done by the parables in the form of visions coming forth from the spiritual mind of the person within the mind of Christ. Things in this life are not square in that they do not line up with the Word of God. God's Word is our straight edge. Everything in our life needs to "square up" with what God says is true. If my body says I am sick, that does not square with God's Word because his Word says, "By his stripes you were healed." These visions have the power to cause my body to square with the truth of God's Word. In other words, these visions have the power to heal my body.

Everything about my life must be made square—everything I think, believe and do must line up perfectly with God's Word. All things must be made right, be adjusted, settled, brought into agreement and made to conform to God's Word. My understanding of my position in him and the course of my life must conform to what God says it is. These parables in the form of visions coming forth from my spiritual mind within the mind of Christ will make all things become square. This is how we will come into the fullness of God. This is also part of the process of this mortal putting on immortality.

Our spiritual interpretation for *When they went, they went upon their four sides* will be as follows:

When these parables in the form of visions coming forth from the mind of Christ within the spiritual mind of the person were leading forth (When they went), they were following a course of action (they went) that would cause everything in this person's life—all thoughts, beliefs, actions and even the physical body—to line up in perfect agreement with the Word of God (upon their four sides).

The next clause, *and they turned not when they went*, was previously examined in verses 9 and 12. It will have the same general meaning here: they were casting away all limitations of earthly existence. The particular application for this verse is that as everything in this person's life becomes square with God's Word, all limitations and earthly boundaries fall away. This is a process.

Putting together all of verse 17 our spiritual interpretation is:

When these parables in the form of visions coming forth from the mind of Christ within the spiritual mind of the person were leading forth (When they went), they were following a course of action (they went) that would cause everything in this person's life—all thoughts, beliefs, actions and even the physical body—to line up in perfect agreement with the Word of God. As everything was coming into perfect alignment with the Word of God, the person was in process for going forth with all limitations of earthly existence removed (and they turned not as they went).

Parable #6

I saw Jesus and myself standing together on a very high mountain peak that gave us a spectacular view of the land below that extended from horizon to horizon. The air was crisp and clear so that visibility was not in the least hindered, and I felt exhilarated by the freshness. It reminded me of my childhood years when my family lived in the Rocky Mountains of Colorado. I used to go on fishing trips with my family...trips that sometimes took us to hidden lakes on mountain peaks that were above timberline. When you are so high that no trees grow, you know you are really up there! As a child, I didn't feel good at that elevation. It gave me a headache and made me feel nauseous. But here with Jesus, even though we were higher than I had ever been, I had none of those feelings. In fact I felt the opposite. Such strength and vitality filled my being that I wanted to leap around from boulder to boulder and even climb up higher. Even though we were extremely high, we had not reached the summit of the mountain and I wanted to continue our climb.

Jesus put one arm around my shoulder and pointed with his other into the distance far to the east. "Do you see that green and brown patch way off there next to the horizon?" I squinted a little trying to adjust my vision toward the spot he was indicating. My eyes finally alighted on the green and brown spot he was indicating.

"What is that?" I asked.

"That is Egypt," he replied. "That is where you came from. You didn't live there long because when you first believed in me at age six, I took you out of there, across the Red Sea, and then you began your journey through the wilderness."

"...the wilderness?" I asked. "You mean I spent my childhood years in a wilderness?"

"Yes," replied Jesus, "and most of your adult years too, but I have been with you every step of the way. Your parents protected you from the many dangers that came against you, but I was in them and you guiding each decision and leading you where I wanted you to be. That is how you came to be here with me today."

Jesus and I sat down together on some boulders that jutted up out of the ground there on the little grassy knoll as we continued enjoying the spectacular view. Looking out over the wilderness into the distance, I saw a road. It wound all over the place. I was aware that the road represented my wilderness wanderings…and wander I did! It was amazing to see how the road went in every conceivable direction…sometimes even in patterns much like the back and forth design of the coils on the back of my old refrigerator.

"That must be where I wavered, halting between two opinions," I mused.

"Yes," said Jesus, "but you finally made the right decisions in the end. You wouldn't be here now if you had not finally made right choices each time you wavered. Have you noticed that even though the road winds a lot, it keeps moving in this direction toward the mountain peak?"

"I see what you mean," I replied, "And the closer it gets to this mountain, the straighter it becomes. I see very few turns in the road now."

"You eventually learned that those distractions that tempted you in the past were not things that could satisfy the longing in your heart for me."

Sometimes it was difficult for me to look at the view because I just wanted to see Jesus. I mostly wanted to look into his eyes. They were the most beautiful blue I had ever seen…bluer than the sky, the delphiniums in my summer garden or the occasional bluebird that flits across the hayfield near our cabin in the mountains of NY. Whenever I looked into his eyes, I felt a deep sense of peace unlike anything I had ever known. There were no problems up here on this mountain. There was nothing to fear or worry about here. I knew that I never wanted to leave this place.

Jesus, knowing my thoughts, said, "You can return to this place anytime you want to because it is in your heart. I am always here waiting for you. Whenever you feel you need a clear perspective on your life, meet me here on this mountain and we will talk about it.

Knowing that Jesus had more to show me about my wilderness road, I forced my eyes back to the scene below.

Jesus continued, "Do you see those places in the road where there are circles? Those are the places where you did not make wise decisions. I made you go around the same experience again until you made the right decision. Sometimes your circumstances changed, but you had to go through the same issues until you responded according to my Word. Then I let you continue moving towards this mountain."

"It all seems so clear to me now," I said. "If only I had understood then what I know now!"

"You understand what you do now, because you went through those experiences," He explained. "Everything was there in my Word to warn you, but much of it you could not receive until you had experiences that made the Word come alive to you."

I thought about that for a moment. How true that had been in my life. There was nothing like a crisis to make the Psalms come to life for me. Whenever I felt alone, hurt or afraid, the Holy Spirit always quickened some portion of his Word to me that gave me direction and took me through.

Looking back at the road, I noticed that not only had it straightened out as I approached the mountain, but also it had been on a steady incline. I had gradually been climbing higher and higher until Jesus did whatever he did that brought me to this high mountain peak with him. As hard as I tried, I could not remember how I got to this high place, so I asked, "Jesus, how did I get to this high mountain with you? I don't remember going up any hairpin curves or climbing up over the cliffs." Looking down from this great height, the climb looked impossible.

Jesus replied, "You learned to use your imagination. That is how you got here. I whispered in your ear that I wanted to meet with you on this high mountain. As you prayed, your heart yearned so deeply to be with me, you began to envision this place and that's how you got here. Your imagination was inspired by me and by your knowledge of my Word. People think the imagination is only for fantasy or things that are not real, but a holy imagination inspired by me, actually brings you into my presence. This is a deep truth that my people in the end times will need to know and practice in order to survive the great trials that are coming upon the earth. "Come, I have more to show you."

With that solemn warning, Jesus arose, held out his hand for me to grasp and led me down a trail that wound around over this plateau on the mountain. Steep rocks jutted up from the mountain on all sides but occasionally we came to small, grassy meadows filled with many varieties and colors of mountain wild flowers. I would like to have stopped to admire these beautiful places, but Jesus indicated we were to continue on. It was not long until we came to a narrow passageway that I can only describe as being a cleft in an enormous rock that towered high above us. This cleft was so narrow that at times we had to turn sideways to slip through. (S. of S. 2:14).

After only a few yards, the passageway opened into a broad place of breathtaking beauty. It was like an oasis. Palm trees soared high into the sky above; flowers abounded everywhere; and immediately in front of us was a deep blue, crystal clear pool of water. We were surrounded by craggy cliffs that made this spectacular place seem totally private. Ferns and delicate flowers were growing out of the cliffs and cascading down the walls in various shades of pink, blue, purple, white and yellow. A sparkling waterfall descended from the top of one of the cliffs into the pool. The fragrance of flowers filled the air.

I stood speechless for a few minutes just drinking in this vast beauty. Then I turned to Jesus and asked, "How can palm trees and an oasis exist on this mountain high above timberline?"

"You are seeing spiritual truth that is not defined by the physical limitations of earth," Jesus replied. "I am the tree of life, the rock, the living water and everything fragrant and lovely you could ever desire. I want you to come here and meet with me often. As you do, you will find healing for your soul and your body. I have more to say to you about this, but first let us go into the water."

I looked down at my hiking boots, blue jeans and long-sleeved plaid shirt. "How can I go swimming in these?" I asked. "I don't have a swimsuit with me."

Jesus gave the biggest smile and almost burst out laughing as he replied, "Just start walking into the water and you will see that it doesn't matter here."

In front of me were stone steps that descended into the water. I did not want to dirty the water with my dusty hiking books, but I knew not to protest and therefore hesitantly began to walk down the steps into the water. As I did so, I found myself clothed in swimming apparel unlike anything I had ever seen on earth. It appeared to be made of a very light-weight, white, filmy material that seemed weightless. It was modest and yet I felt totally unrestricted in any movement.

The water was warm and inviting. There was a feeling of total rest in the water as there was no need to work at staying afloat. I could swim and float on my back, but if I chose to remain upright without moving my arms and legs, I did not sink although I could not touch the bottom.

I had not seen Jesus enter the water, but he was there and motioned to me to come over to where he was in a small alcove of the pool. There the water was even warmer and it churned in a massaging kind of way like a hot tub on earth but much gentler.

"If you will come here often and talk with me, you will find healing for your body," Jesus said. "Do you remember the promise I made to my people when they were wandering in the wilderness and stopped at Marah just before going to Elim?"

"Yes, I remember," I replied excitedly. "I have been studying and meditating on that passage. I even memorized the promise because I wanted it to be mine."

Jesus smiled as he looked at me. He had asked me the question knowing full well that I had been working that through in my mind for quite some time now and had memorized the passage. "Well, what does that promise say?" he asked.

I recited, "If thou wilt diligently hearken to the voice of the LORD thy God, and wilt do that which is right in his sight, and wilt give ear to his commandments, and keep all his statutes, I will put none of these diseases upon thee, which I have brought upon the Egyptians: for I am the LORD that healeth thee."

"That is one of the most important healing scriptures in the whole Bible," he commented. "It shows there is a correlation between a person's relationship with me and freedom of disease or sicknesses of any kind. It is never my desire for anyone to be sick, and I could heal everyone when they ask for I have the power to do so. However, it would not be in their best interest for me to do so."

"I think I understand," I commented. "When things are going well for us in life, we tend to get caught up in the busyness of life and neglect our relationship with you. People don't realize that knowing you will give them greater joy, fulfillment and excitement than anything on earth could ever provide."

"Yes," Jesus affirmed with a look of longing in his eyes. "I have so much to give my people if they would only turn their focus from worldly pursuits to me."

"Sometimes that is hard for me to do," I lamented. "Even though I have learned that I can meet with you in lovely places like this, I can still get distracted by the pull of television. It is so 'in your face'. Sometimes it takes all the self control I can muster to walk away from the TV and go to the visions within as you have taught me. I think I'm doing much better with that though."

"Yes, you are," he agreed. "Your flesh is attracted to those things and it needs to die, but we are working on that…and it is going" he added.

"Another thing I struggle with" I continued, "is all I have to do each day. I want to spend more time with you but so many tasks are calling for me to do them, I don't know which one to do first and there is no way everything can get done."

"If you will ask me what you are to do next throughout your day, I will lead you. That is what I mean by telling you in my Word that if you will hearken to my voice and obey me, I will not allow you to suffer disease. Obeying my commandments as laid out in my Word is important and part of that is learning to listen to my voice throughout your day. I want to be a part of everything you do, and your asking me about each decision helps keep my presence in your conscious mind and will result in your deeper joy, greater productivity, and better health. Think about how different last Thursday would have been if you had done this."

I didn't want to think about last Thursday in this beautiful place. I felt totally relaxed as the warm water swirled around massaging my whole body. I floated on my back and looked up at the deep blue sky just in time to see an eagle soaring around in the heavenlies, his wings tipped with glimmering gold from the glorious light that filled that place. Everything was bathed in light, and a sweet fragrance filled the air. Even though there were flowers all around, I knew the fragrance came from Jesus as also did the light.

I looked again into Jesus' face and it was even lovelier than our surroundings, lovely because of things difficult to describe…his look of love and acceptance towards me, the holiness and wisdom that exuded from his presence. How can one describe the face of God? I can only imagine as I see myself there in his presence.

"Awe, yes," last Thursday," I said reluctantly. "That was not a good day for me."

My husband and I had been at our little cabin in the mountains of New York, a place we visit whenever our schedules permit. That morning I had experienced an allergy attack like I used to have years ago before Jesus healed me of hay fever. It was fall and the weather had changed, both of which were conditions that used to sometimes render me incapable of doing anything but blow my nose and sneeze! I could not understand why I was having this trouble again.

I knew what I was to do to overcome it. I went in my mind to one of the lovely places inside that I have developed over the years with Jesus' help. I went to the healing river and spent time with him there talking over the healing scriptures and letting him heal me. After a time there, I felt fine.

Then my husband said that he had been on his computer checking the weather report for our area. It was supposed to frost that night…almost a month earlier than we would have expected. We have a big garden there and it was full of produce that needed to be harvested. We were intending to leave that morning and head back to our home in the city where we had appointments and work to be done, but that garden had to be taken care of immediately…or so I thought.

I quickly put on my gardening clothes and set to work in the garden while my husband mowed the yard one last time. I was miserable. It was pick a squash…blow my nose. Pick some peppers, blow my nose. I had a terrible time getting done the things that needed to be done. All the while I was asking God why I had lost the victory I had gained earlier that morning. When I returned to the city and began ministering to people, I was fine.

The next day in the city started out just as the day before. As I sat praying early in the morning, my nose started running again. I went to one of my healing places with Jesus and then I was fine. The next thing I did, however, was to ask him what he wanted me to do next. I felt impressed that I was to write more of the vision I have been slowly putting on paper. This I began to do. I was fine for the entire day. The weather was the same, the pollen was just as thick, but nothing was bothering me. I knew the difference was that I had asked Jesus what he wanted me to do and then obeyed.

"It is taking time for you to learn this," Jesus said smiling, "but you will come to the time when you will not order your day without first asking me what I want you to do. You don't have to ask me what you can wear or if you can eat lunch. What I am trying to teach you is how to manage your schedule so you can accomplish all that I have asked you to do. I realize I have put a lot on your shoulders, but as long as you are in me and I am in you, you can accomplish it all. I would never ask you to do more than you are able to do. As long as you don't try to do things on your own without asking me, I will lead you and empower you."

I knew this was true. If I had stopped and asked God what he wanted me to do before charging out to the garden in haste, he would have helped me with the work. Maybe my husband would have finished mowing sooner than expected and come to help sooner than he did. I knew now that I was supposed to do more writing before working in the garden that morning. I also knew that my miserable day would serve as a good reminder to ask Jesus before determining what I would do each day.

"It is very important for you to write these visions," Jesus said seriously. "My people need to know how to come to me in the difficult days that lie ahead for this world. As the economy is shaken, health care will also be shaken. I want my people to walk in health. I also want them to trust in me rather than in science and doctors. Every one of my people is at a different stage in their walk of faith, but all will be called to walk at a deeper level with me than they have ever known as things they have trusted in crumble around them. Some will gradually be led away from their reliance on medical science. Others will be immediately cut off from it because of their finances. Medicines are becoming polluted. I want my people to ask me before getting an injection or putting medicine into their body. I will lead them if they will only ask me. Trusting me for all their health is a process that my people must be pressing into. The visions will help them grow closer to me in relationship and bring healing to their bodies.

As I thought about what Jesus was saying, I was so thankful he had led me into having visions because I knew my relationship with him had come to a whole new dimension through them. They came as a result of my study and meditation of the Word. I chose to envision the Word to the best of my ability. As I did so, I became aware that Jesus was helping me with this. They became alive and I felt Jesus' presence as I pictured him in my mind according to Scripture. Many spiritual realities are given in earthly types so we can understand and experience spiritual truth on our level. As I was thinking about the beauty of all this Jesus said,

"This water represents the living water of my Spirit and my Word. When you come here in your mind to be with me in this pool, you are immersing yourself in me."

I looked down into the water that was swirling around us. Never had I seen anything as pure and clear as this, and yet I could not see the bottom of the pool.

Jesus knowing my thoughts said, "There are no limits in me. No matter how deeply you study my Word, there will always be another deeper level to be uncovered. No matter how much of my Spirit dwells within you, there is always more for you to receive." Jesus cupped his hands, scooped up some of the water and held it to my face, "Here, drink this," he said.

As I drank the water I felt my whole being coming into a new dimension of revelation--like it was being awakened. The water swirling around my body suddenly felt like love. There was gentleness in the water along with rest, goodness, love, peace and even joy. I could feel it all in and through my body!

I want more of this, I exclaimed as I submerged my head and dove down deeper into the water.

When I came back to the surface, Jesus was laughing as he said, "O, my Beloved, I have so much for you. It gives me such joy to give to my people, but they must come to me and see me before I can do these things for them."

Jesus, indicating I was to follow him, swam over to a big, flat rock in the center of the pool closer to the waterfall. We climbed up onto the rock and lay on our backs as we looked up at the deep blue sky. Little fluffy, white clouds skirted across the expanse changing shape as they moved. For a few minutes we talked about what the different shapes reminded us of--a game I used to play as a child. Then Jesus said, "You have a question about my healing promise you memorized from Exodus 15."

"Yes, I do," I replied. "You say you will keep us free from disease if we will hearken to your voice, do what is right in your sight, and obey all your commandments and all your statutes. How can I possibly do all that? I keep forgetting or messing up in some way. I am far from being able to do all that. I don't see how anyone could live so perfectly."

"I understand how you feel," Jesus said smiling at me with love and understanding in his eyes." "You know my love for you will never change and is not based on anything you do, but walking in divine health will require your total cooperation and submission to me. The key to this lies in the verses that precede the one you memorized. It is always important to notice the context in which my promises are given. What do you remember about the preceding verses?"

I replied, "Your people journeyed in the wilderness for three days without finding water. Finally they came to a place called Marah where there was water but it was so bitter they could not drink it. The people grumbled and complained. Then Moses prayed and you told him to cast a tree into the water. When he did, it became sweet.

"What do you think that means?" Jesus asked.

"Marah means 'bitter' and represents circumstances in our life that are painful and difficult," I replied. "The tree is a type of the cross. When we face difficulties in life, if we will choose to accept your will rather than our own, we will die to self and your life will be formed in us."

"That's it!" Jesus exclaimed. "That is the key. As you die to self, my life will be formed in you and I will guide your decisions and enable you to fully obey all my commandments. You must yield yourself to me, lean on me, and I will live through you. I want you to become so one with me that your life will be lived together with mine as though we are one person. My people living in these end times will be enabled to do this more fully than all those have lived before you, but they must accept my cross. Without the cross, there will be no power, and living free of disease will require my power in your life."

As I lay there on the big, flat rock with Jesus talking about the Scriptures and feeling the warm sun on my body, I sensed new strength permeating my being. Both my soul and my body were being healed and renewed in his presence in this lovely place. I knew what Jesus was telling me was of utmost importance. I also knew it was vitally imperative that his people learn to come to lovely places like this to be with him. I remember how difficult it had been for me to train my mind to focus on visualizing our relationship and the Scriptures.

"You have found a priceless treasure by learning to come here," Jesus said. "The time you spend taking every thought captive to me and casting down your vain imaginations will help keep your mind in perfect peace as the evil intensifies in these end times. When great fear comes upon the world, you will be able to stand against it by coming to the places of peace within where you have learned to find my strength and presence. I want you to tell my people about this. They must all learn to find me in the secret places of their heart. The very lives of my people are going to depend solely on their relationship with me. I will heal their bodies. I will provide food and shelter for them. I will heat their homes in the cold of winter, but they must give up everything for me."

I looked into Jesus eyes and said, "Lord, I will do everything I can to encourage others to find you in this way. I feel I must go now and continue writing the vision so others will learn about visions and perhaps gain the confidence to find you in this way themselves."

"I will be with you as you write," Jesus promised. "and my power will enable others to do this as they take the time to seek me and meditate on my Word. And remember," he added, "You can come here any time throughout your day and I will be waiting."

Verse 18 – The Spiritual Body Feels God's Touch
As for their rings, they were so high that they were dreadful; and their rings were full of eyes round about them four.

A new word is introduced here, "rings" or *gab* in the Hebrew. Because this word is so complex and the revelation that comes with it so astounding, we need to look at the entire definition as it appears in Strong's.

Rings - 1354. gab, gab; from an unused root mean. to hollow or curve; the back (as rounded [comp. H1460 and H1479]; by anal. the top or rim, a boss, a vault, arch of - eye, bulwarks, etc.:—back, body, boss, eminent (higher) place, [eye] brows, nave, ring.

We will use several of Strong's definitions to arrive at our spiritual understanding of this word including "body," "back," "eminent (higher) place," "nave" and "ring."

The "rings" refer specifically to the spiritual body. We see "body" in the definition. In addition to this, it has been in "back" of the body so to speak where it was not seen. It is "higher" or more "eminent" than the physical body.

In previous verses we learned that we have two bodies, one natural and one spiritual, and that as part of the process of coming into perfection, these two bodies are to be separated by the word of God coming forth from the mind of Christ within the spiritual mind of the person. Now we will learn more about the spiritual body itself. The first thing we learn about it is that once it has been separated from the natural body, it is free to experience the love of God in a new dimension.

The spiritual body has senses just the same as the natural body—these senses include seeing, hearing, smelling, tasting and feeling. This verse tells us the rings, the spiritual body, is full of eyes. The Hebrew word for eyes, 'ayin, also means "knowledge." The spiritual body is full of knowledge. And just what is this knowledge? As we shall see, it is the knowledge that the person is totally loved by God. Only one of the five senses can be known all over the body and that is the sense of feeling. When the spiritual body has been separated from the natural body, it is free to feel the love of God, a feeling that permeates the entire body in such a way that every cell of the spiritual body deeply feels the love of Christ.

At this point, the person feels this love as though the natural body is experiencing it. The two bodies have been separated but they are still so closely connected it is difficult to know which is which. It is like what Paul experienced when he said, "Whether in the body, I cannot tell; or whether out of the body, I cannot tell" (2 Cor. 12:2). Then Paul repeats in verse three, "whether in the body, or out of the body, I cannot tell: God knoweth."

There is absolutely no experience of floating near the ceiling looking down on one's body. Remember, only one of the senses has been awakened—the sense of feeling—and the bodies are closely connected. The spiritual eyes and ears are gradually awakening as we envision parables, but the sense of feeling is the strongest and it is constant.

Experiencing God's love is absolutely essential for coming into his fullness. At this point of spiritual development, we are living the reality of Paul's prayer in Ephesians 3. We are beginning to know the love of Christ in a way that surpasses all knowledge because it has gone beyond knowledge to feeling. The depth of love expressed here is far beyond intellectual understanding or mere words.

Feeling God's Touch

In this new realm of spirit the parables take on a new dimension. Now when one imagines Christ touching one's face, his touch is actually felt. When he anoints the person's head with oil, they feel the warm oil flowing down over their head. However, feeling his presence in the body is not limited to the time spent visualizing the parables; it is a constant, pulsating, warm love felt all over the body in a way that defies description. We will be like Paul when he spoke of hearing unspeakable words. In this level of spiritual increase, we will not be permitted to speak about many things we are experiencing.

As we continue with our definitions, we will find a "ring," *gab*, is also defined by Strong as a "nave." A nave is the hub of a wheel. The hub is in the center of a wheel. What would be in the center of the mind of Christ (wheel)? The hub is the place on the wheel where the spokes are attached as they go out to the rim of the wheel thereby giving it strength and support. What would be the very center of all the activity of God from which every spoke goes forth? Would it not be love? Isn't our God totally motivated by love?

The Bible reveals God and his purpose and plan for us from all eternity. In the Bible we see the mind of Christ revealed. Every eternal truth revealed in God's Word is like the spoke of a wheel in the mind of God coming forth from the motivational center of pure love.

Another meaning for "ring" given by Strong is "bulwark." In Isa. 26:1, we are told that salvation is a bulwark thus giving us a connection between salvation and bulwark. Our experience of feeling God's love in this new dimension is part of coming into full salvation.

In the natural, a ring is something circular having no beginning or end and is often given to a loved one during the marriage ceremony as a symbol of undying love.

Putting together all of the above we can say that the "rings" are the spiritual body that has been separated from the natural body. This spiritual body, now that it is no longer united with the physical body, is free to experience the love of God as an actual feeling that permeates every part. The knowledge that one is deeply loved by God is no longer just head knowledge but is deeply felt all over the entire body. When one envisions being touched by God, one can feel God's touch at the place envisioned.

As we experience this great depth of love continually, an incredible sense of deep, reverential awe comes over us. Our understanding of this great love opens to us a knowledge and understanding never before known. We begin to see everything in our life from the perspective of God's perfect love. Everything that ever happened to us (things that have a beginning or things that are made [four]) will now be seen in the context of God's perfect love. All of life (material things and matter itself) will now be understood as being given from a loving heavenly Father whose only intent was to bring us unto himself for love and blessing. This will completely change all the erroneous thinking and judging that inevitably arise from our responses to life and that have hindered our ability to know God.

I am reminded of something a friend recently shared with me. Her daughter, now an adult, had been rebellious and immoral as a teenager thereby breaking her mother's heart. The daughter eventually married and gave birth to her own baby girl. She then came to her mother and apologized for the grief she had caused her mother. She explained that the love she felt for her own baby was far beyond any love she had ever believed possible. Now she understood how much her own mother loved her and how she had grieved her. She was seeing her entire past from a different perspective—the perspective of love. Now she understood.

All of us at some point have doubted God's love for us. As we have experienced the inevitable disappointments and pain of life, we have wrongly interpreted our circumstances and misjudged God's intentions. As we come into the fullness, all this must go. Paul prayed in Ephesians 3, that we would be rooted and grounded in love and that we might know the breadth, length, depth, and height of the love of Christ that surpasses all knowledge that we might be filled with the fullness of God. Only as God brings to us a revelation of his perfect love will we be able to come into perfection. The separation of the spiritual body from the natural body will enable this knowledge of God's love to permeate all of our being in a way never before known by humankind.

Before writing our spiritual interpretation of this verse, we need to examine a few more Hebrew words.

The word, "high," is from a root word meaning "lofty." Webster says "lofty" means noble and sublime. Sublime means majestic, inspiring awe or admiration through grandeur or beauty.

"Dreadful," *yir'ah*, means "fear" and "reverence." This word is used throughout the Old Testament in terms of the fear of God.

The Bible tells us, "The fear of the Lord is the beginning of knowledge" (Prov. 1:7) and "The fear of the LORD is the beginning of wisdom: and the knowledge of the holy is understanding" (Prov. 9:10).

Putting together all of the above, our spiritual interpretation of the first clause is:

As for the spiritual body (As for the rings), it was lifted up into a very high and majestic place inspiring feelings of grandeur, awe, and reverence for God far above anything these persons had ever known (they were so high that they were dreadful);

This leads us into our next clause:

...their rings were full of eyes round about them four.

171

In Hebrew, "eyes," *'ayin*, also means "knowledge."

"Round about" also means "environs," or "on every side."

"Four" will mean here, "man in his relation to the world as created. It is the number of things that have a beginning, of things that are made, of material things, and matter itself."

Our spiritual interpretation for the second clause of this verse reads as follows:

In this high and exalted place, their spiritual body was able to feel the love of Jesus Christ in every part (their rings were full of eyes). The enormity and wonder of this awesome experience caused them to see all of life—everything that ever happened to them and everything in their environment—from a perspective of God's continuous, unfailing and perfect love (round about them four).

At this point we will bring together our entire interpretation of verse 18:

As for the spiritual body (As for the rings), it was lifted up into a very high and majestic place inspiring feelings of grandeur, awe, and reverence for God far above anything these persons had ever known (they were so high that they were dreadful); In this high and exalted place their spiritual body was able to feel the love of Jesus Christ in every part (their rings were full of eyes). The enormity and wonder of this awesome experience caused them to see all of life—everything that ever happened to them and everything in their environment—from a perspective of God's continuous, unfailing and perfect love (round about them four).

My Experience

I would like to share now some of the things I have felt of the Lord's presence that could only have been felt by my spiritual body being awakened. It takes a spiritual body to feel the Holy Spirit's touch. Before this experience, I was not a person who felt much of anything of a spiritual nature. I could go to church services where people were crying, laughing, falling under the

Spirit's power, seeing visions or whatever, and I felt nothing. I used to wonder why I didn't experience any of the things that others seemed to feel. Well, all that has changed! I feel the Lord all the time. It is incredible and totally awesome beyond my ability to describe!

The following are some of the things I have felt. These were initiated by Jesus and not a result of a parable I envisioned.

Brenda had a vision that Jesus was pouring anointing oil over my head. The next day I started feeling the oil coming down over my head over and over again all day long. It is not like what the physical body would feel in that it wasn't oily or wet feeling. It was spiritual and that is difficult to explain. It was an awesome feeling though and it lasted for about one day.

In another of her visions, the Lord was brushing my hair back out of my face. I began to feel this thirteen years ago, and I still feel it! Whenever I am quiet and think about him, I feel him gently brushing my hair back on the left side of my face. I also feel his breath upon my cheek on the other side of my face. It feels warm and moist and has the regular rhythm of breathing. These two manifestations of his presence, along with the feelings of my spiritual body having been awakened, are always with me.

I often hear his heart beating. Sometimes when I am very still, I can feel the rise and fall of his chest very near me as he breathes. Many times I have felt his tears on one side of my face. I sometimes feel his hand on my shoulder. This usually comes when I am studying the Bible or writing. It is very, very gentle. I have often felt him as the sun shining on my face. This feeling lasts for a few minutes and then fades away.

All that I have felt of the Lord has been characterized by extreme gentleness. He is always warm. He moves slowly. The stroking of my hair back from my face is very gentle and slow. These are only a few of the ways I have felt his presence.

All of these sensations are telling me that Jesus is very near and that he loves me. Since I have been feeling some of these things every day for thirteen years now, I also know that he will never leave me…not even for a second. I have known this previously because his Word tells me this is so, but having the actual truth of this demonstrated continually for thirteen years is lifting me to a whole new dimension of faith. It will be important for us to feel his presence in the days to come when terror reigns on earth. The Spirit witnesses to my spirit that what is coming on earth will cause sheer panic beyond anything we have ever known. Jesus will be our only hope and we must be able to experience him in a supernatural dimension. The fact that he has revealed to me a last days' message from the four living creatures and allowed me to feel these things and given me permission to write them all suggest to me that great tribulation is almost upon us. We are definitely in the very last of the last days, and we must do everything possible to be prepared spiritually for what is coming.

Someone might be wondering how I know this is Jesus and not some other spirit. I know because of the tremendous peace, love, and gentleness of his nearness. I know because of the fruit in my life and the way the Word is opened to me daily as I study. I no longer have wilderness periods where the Bible seems dry and uninteresting. The Word is always alive to me. Jesus shows me things every day. I have peace in my soul. The total constancy of this experience speaks to me of God's promises to never leave us or forsake us. It speaks of his unchangeableness. He is the same yesterday, today and forever and I feel that. I know because of the crosses I have experienced. The more we die to self, the less we can be deceived. And lastly, I know because I am under my husband's authority and I stay closely connected to the body of believers God has placed in my life. They are very discerning people and they tell me when the slightest little thing is off kilter in my life. Although our experiences with Jesus are very personal, we must always retain a certain transparency in our relationships in the body of believers to which we have been called. We are not crossing over by ourselves but we are crossing together as a body. I cannot over emphasize this important fact.

Another Kind of Knowledge (Eyes)

Along with love, there is another knowledge that comes when our spiritual body has been awakened. This involves hearing from God through our body. We are like a newborn baby...as though we have just been born into the kingdom of God. A newborn infant doesn't see very well. It doesn't understand language yet, but it understands feeling. It knows it is loved when it is held close in its mother or father's arms because it feels that love with its body. It knows that a touch on its cheek signals that the breast is near for nourishment. When it is placed in its bed, it is time for sleep.

In our spiritual development with an awakened "newborn" spiritual body, God speaks to us through our body. Here are some of the ways I have learned to hear him. When I am thinking about something and I feel a very warm flush come over my face and spread out over my body (this is a different feeling from the sunshine I sometimes feel on my face), I know Jesus is saying "yes" or "everything will be okay." This happens totally at his volition. I can't just ask him a question and expect him to answer in this way. No, it happens when I least expect it. I am just thinking about something, and this feeling comes that speaks volumes to me. For example, I may be trying to find a pair of shoes that fit. My feet are difficult to fit but I have experienced several times trying on a pair of shoes and feeling that warm flush spread over me. I know then that I have found the right pair of shoes! Or I can be trying to find something at home and I'm wondering if the item for which I am searching may no longer be in my possession, if I feel this warm flush, I know to keep looking and I will find the item.

God also has a way of telling me "no" or "something is not right here." I have a certain tooth that gives a little jab of pain when God is saying this. Someone may be saying something that is not accurate. I'll feel that jab in my tooth and I know not to accept what is being said. I have been to the dentist several times to have that tooth checked, and he always says there is nothing wrong with it. I know it is just a tool God uses to teach me.

Another way he has of saying "no" to me is through coughing. I may be trying to say something and a sudden fit of coughing will make it impossible for me to speak. Then I realize God didn't want me to say that particular thing.

God will tell me "no" with sneezing. If I start to do something and have a sudden outburst of sneezes, I know God doesn't want me doing that thing. He has taught me many things just through the signals of "yes" and "no." I want to add here that I don't believe everyone's experience with feeling God's touch will be the same as what I have described here. We are all different and God has unlimited ways of communicating with us via touch.

Verse 19 - The Soul Is Now Under the Spirit's Control
And when the living creatures went, the wheels went by them: and when the living creatures were lifted up from the earth, the wheels were lifted up.

Some of the above words are not in the original Hebrew. The words we can view in Strong's Concordance are *living creatures went, wheels went, living creatures were lifted up earth, wheels were lifted up.*

Once again, the Hebrew word for "went" is *yalak,* a verb we have encountered many times in our Ezekiel passage. For this verse the definitions we will use for *yalak* are "followed" and "led forth."

Our spiritual interpretation of *And when the living creatures went, the wheels went by them* will be:

The mature Christians who were having this experience with God of coming into perfection (the living creatures) were following (went) wherever the mind of Christ within their own spiritual mind (the wheels) led them (went).

This is a description of persons who are totally led by the Holy Spirit. They do nothing of their own volition but only move as the Spirit directs. There is no more struggle between the flesh and the spirit concerning who is in charge. Their will is totally submitted to Jesus Christ. The last half of verse 19 will explain why this is so.

...and when the living creatures were lifted up from the earth, the wheels were lifted up.

As we learned in verse 15, the "earth" is the soul. Here we see these mature Christians being lifted up above their soul. The soul, that part of our being that is subject to impure motives and selfishness, is now in a position subservient to the spirit. The separation of soul and spirit has enabled the spiritual mind within the mind of Christ to be lifted up into a higher position. (Although there has been a separation of soul and spirit, there is still an attachment but the soul's dominance has been greatly reduced.)

Here is our spiritual interpretation for the last half of this verse:

These mature Christians were lifted up from their soul so that it was now in a low position where it could no longer dominate or control their lives (and when the living creatures were lifted up from the earth). The spiritual mind within the mind of Christ was lifted up into its rightful place of leadership and dominance (the wheels were lifted up.)

These believers are now perfectly aligned with the Holy Spirit in everything they think and do. Almost every motive is pure because it is not coming from the soul but from their spirit joined with the spirit of Christ. At this point, they are still human and sin is still a possibility, but the spirit is dominant and the will is almost totally submitted to the complete lordship of Christ. The people who have progressed to this point are the ones who have been willing to be that grain of wheat that falls into the ground and dies that it may bear much fruit. They are able to say with Christ, "My meat is to do the will of him that sent me, and to finish his work."

When believers reach this stage of the fullness, they will be in almost perfect unity one with another. They will soon be that mighty army in Joel that does not break ranks; the earth will quake before them and the heavens will tremble. With this level of holiness, God will be able to pour in his power to accomplish his end time plans because he knows the power will not be misused. These people will not minister in order to gain a reputation, be adored by people, or amass wealth because they have died to self and the soul is in a lower position than the spirit.

At this point, they may be hidden away, unrecognized by anyone, but God's power is working within them to bring them completely into his fullness. Much has been accomplished in their lives, but there is still more to be done before they begin their great end time ministry.

The following is our interpretation of verse 19 in its entirety:

The mature Christians who were having this experience with God of coming into perfection (the living creatures) were following (went) wherever the mind of Christ within their own spiritual mind (the wheels) led them (went). These mature Christians were lifted up from their soul so that it was now in a low position where it could no longer dominate or control their lives (and when the living creatures were lifted up from the earth). The spiritual mind within the mind of Christ was lifted up into its rightful place of leadership and dominance (the wheels were lifted up).

Chapter Eleven
The Four Living Creatures in Heaven

Verse 20 - Entering the Presence of the Father
Whithersoever the spirit was to go, they went, thither was their spirit to go; and the wheels were lifted up over against them: for the spirit of the living creature was in the wheels.

There comes a time in our spiritual transformation when the Holy Spirit takes us into the presence of the Father as this verse reveals.

The first word in this verse, whithersoever, is an interesting word. It is used frequently in the scriptures and has a wide extent of meaning. In most instances it is used as a preposition, a word that would not seem very important in discerning the deep spiritual meaning of a passage. However, here in this verse it seems to stand out, perhaps because it is the first word.

Strong tells us the Hebrew word for "whithersoever," *'al*, is the same as another word, *'al,* but used as a preposition. This other word means "to Jehovah" or "the Highest." This will be used in part of our spiritual interpretation of this word. The other part will come from Gesenius who tells us one meaning of this word is as follows:

> 'al - above—when anything is put on the upper part of another, so as to stand or lie upon it, or have it for its substratum—used of the state of rest, e.g. to lie…on a bed

The next word is "spirit," which I believe refers to the Holy Spirit. The second word for "spirit" is referring to the human spirit. We know that the human spirit and the Holy Spirit have become one spirit. Now the human spirit has come into complete rest, relying totally on the Holy Spirit for all things. This is now possible because the spirit is no longer connected to the soul. This word, whithersoever, gives us a lovely picture of our spirit lying upon the spirit of Christ. We are united as one but at the same time we are distinct personalities like a husband and wife. In this state of rest, we go in our spirit wherever the spirit of Christ leads. The word, 'al, indicates where the spirit is going—up to the highest God, up to Jehovah. This indicates rising higher in our comprehension of God the Father and into a deeper revelation of the Trinity.

In the previous verse these mature believers were following wherever the mind of Christ within their mind led them. In this verse they are going wherever the Spirit leads them. The latter part of this verse then concludes that the spirits are within the minds.

The word "thither" means "in it."

Our spiritual interpretation for first part of this verse is as follows:

Whenever the Holy Spirit ascended up to the highest place before God the Father (whithersoever the spirit was to go), the mature Christians also went up into this most high place (they went). They were able to do this because their spirit was joined with the Spirit of Christ in a position of perfect rest (thither was their spirit to go).

The last half of verse 20 states, *and the wheels were lifted up over against them: for the spirit of the living creature was in the wheels.*

"Over against" means "near" or "beside."

As the spirits were lifted up, the minds were also lifted up beside them (and the wheels were lifted up over against them) because the spirit of the persons united with the Spirit of Christ was within their mind that was within the mind of Christ (for the spirit of the living creature was in the wheels).

In the first part of verse 19 the mature Christians were following wherever the mind of Christ led them. Because these people had been willing to die to the things of this world in every aspect of their lives, they were ready to be lifted up above their soul. This lifting up from the soul brings them into a whole new dimension of spirit. The spirit unencumbered by the soul is able to soar up into the highest heaven even as Paul when he spoke of being caught up into paradise and hearing unspeakable words.

If the spirit is within the mind, then the spirit goes wherever the mind leads. This means that when my mind is envisioning being in a lovely place in heaven with Jesus, my spirit actually goes there. Now we are getting a picture of how the parables formed in the imagination of the mind are able to transport the spirit any place the mind can think of. This ability comes only after the spirit is lifted up above the soul.

Now when I envision being in a lovely meadow graced with fragrant flowers and the gentle breezes of heaven caressing my skin, my spirit is actually there. And since my spirit is joined with the spirit of Christ, Jesus is there with me. I have been transported in spirit into heaven. It is important to remember this is not spirit travel such as reported by people involved in occult practices. This is not talking about geographical travel in space to someplace "out there." This is only a different dimension of human experience with God. If a person is sitting in a chair in the living room communing with God and envisioning a heavenly parable, that person is seeing something in the mind and feeling it in the body, but there is still the awareness of being in the living room.

It might seem more logical to us to think of our mind as being within our spirit, but it is clear from this passage that our spirit is within our mind. Eph. 4:23 confirms this, "And be renewed in the spirit of your mind." Knowing that the spirit is in the mind will greatly facilitate our understanding about how God desires to work in us to draw us into a deeper revelation of himself in these end times.

There are limitations to our mind because when original sin occurred, the curse came upon all parts of our being including our mind. As a result, we must labor in our mind to learn through study, memorization, etc. Some people have a much higher intelligence quotient than others, but all of us have limitations. However, in our imagination we can become anything we want, go anyplace we desire, work miracles, or as Webster defines imagination, "create mental images of what is not actually present or what has never been created or experienced." If we combine imagination with the definition of faith in Heb. 11:1,

"Now faith is the substance of things hoped for, the evidence of things not seen," we can see that the imagination plays an important part in our ability to have faith and believe for the unseen or unrealized.

There is a vast portion of our mind we don't use. Since the spirit is in the mind and the spirit is without limitation, it is easy to see that this unused portion of the mind, once activated by God in the end times, can bring us into depths of spirit never before known to humankind.

Here is our spiritual interpretation of verse 20 in its entirety:

Whenever the Holy Spirit ascended up to the highest place before God the Father (whithersoever the spirit was to go), the mature Christians also went up into this most high place (they went). They were able to do this because their spirit was joined with the Spirit of Christ in a position of perfect rest (thither was their spirit to go). As the spirits were lifted up, the minds were also lifted up beside them (and the wheels were lifted up over against them) because the spirit of the persons united with the Spirit of Christ was within their mind that was within the mind of Christ (for the spirit of the living creature was in the wheels).

Around the Throne

We can see these living creatures as they have ascended into heaven in Christ in Revelation 4.

The KJV calls them four "beasts" but other translations refer to them as "four living creatures" or "four living beings," terms that most commentators agree are more appropriate than "beasts." The fact that the number four is used with these living creatures informs us they are related to God's creation, specifically the earth. We see in Revelation 6 that whenever they speak, it is concerning matters on earth as they say, "Come and see." They are the mature Christians who are still on earth but also have realized their position in heaven as they have been taken into the very throne room of God.

Most commentators agree that these are the same living creatures described in Ezekiel. If this is true, then it follows, as we have been learning from our study, that they are on earth in the end times but have also ascended into heaven.

John, the one who experienced and wrote The Revelation, is the disciple of whom Jesus said, "If I will that he tarry till I come, what is that to thee?" The scripture continues by saying, "Then went this saying abroad among the brethren, that that disciple should not die: yet Jesus said not unto him, He shall not die; but, If I will that he tarry till I come, what is that to thee?" (John 21:22,23)

John is a type of those who will enter into this great revelation of the four living creatures—those who are on earth at the coming of Christ...those who will tarry till he comes and will not die. John sees them in heaven in Revelation 4.

> And before the throne there was a sea of glass like unto crystal: and in the midst of the throne, and round about the throne, were four beasts full of eyes before and behind. And the first beast was like a lion, and the second beast like a calf, and the third beast had a face as a man, and the fourth beast was like a flying eagle (Rev 4:6, 7).

Here is the same verse in the New International Version which I like because it uses the words "living creatures" rather than "beasts."

> In the center, around the throne, were four living creatures, and they were covered with eyes, in front and in back. The first living creature was like a lion, the second was like an ox, the third had a face like a man, the fourth was like a flying eagle (NIV).

The first thing mentioned about them is "they were covered with eyes, in front and in back." This can be explained according to our study of Ezek. 1:18 where we learned the rings were the spiritual body. It was full of eyes, meaning full of the knowledge of God's love. So this first statement identifies them with the four living creatures of Ezekiel 1.

In Revelation as in Ezekiel, numbers are not giving us numerical information but rather spiritual meaning. Just as there are not literally four living creatures in Ezekiel, there are not four different living creatures in Revelation. The number four only tells us they are related to earth, God's creation.

The number "first" informs us that these living creatures cannot be divided. They are unified in heart and purpose. "There is one body, and one Spirit, even as ye are called in one hope of your calling; One Lord, one faith, one baptism, One God and Father of all, who is above all, and through all, and in you all" (Eph. 4:4-6).

The word "lion" in this passage again refers to Jesus, the lion of the tribe of Judah. We see that the living creatures are unified in being one with Jesus and inseparable from him. Their unity with him insures their unity with one another.

To understand what "second" means, we need to look again at Bullinger. Before in our study, the number two was indicating division and difference, "The second of any number of things always bears upon it the stamp of difference, and generally of enmity," but Bullinger goes on to say,

> ...where there are two, though there is still difference, this difference may be in a good sense. It may be for...association and mutual help. It may be the proverbial 'Two and two' of apostleship and service. Or it may be our association with Christ in death and resurrection. The second person of the Trinity partook of two natures—perfect God and perfect man. Two are better than one, because they have a good reward for their labour. For if they fall, the one will lift up his fellow; but woe to him that is alone when he falleth, for he hath not another to help him up. Two testimonies may be different, but yet one may support, strengthen and corroborate the other. Jesus said: "The testimony of two men is true. I am one that bear witness of myself, and the Father that sent me beareth witness of me" (John 8:17,18). God's own revelation is two-fold. The Old Covenant and the New are God's sufficient testimony to man. And yet how different. The Law and Grace; Faith and Works! We may notice also that it is the second Person of the Trinity who is specially called "the Faithful Witness" (Rev. 1:5). And we have other examples of the number Two in connection with faithful

testimony. Caleb and Joshua were two faithful witnesses of the truth of God's Word." (Bullinger 1967, 104-5)

This number "second" indicates many things about these living creatures. They are different from others in heaven in that they still have a natural body but they are assisting one another in accomplishing God's work on earth. They have participated in Christ's death and resurrection in their own lives. They bear witness of Christ upon the earth and their witness is true and faithful. They are like the beloved in Song of Solomon, "What will ye see in the Shulamite? As it were the company of two armies" (Song 6:13b). The living creatures are leading the army on earth while at the same time working with the army in heaven.

They are like a calf. We saw in Ezekiel that they had the face, or heart, of an ox with ox being representative of their soul. When we see them in Revelation the ox has become a calf. An ox is a beast of burden because of its great strength. A calf does not have the strength of an adult ox. This shows that although these living creatures still have a soul, the soul is no longer strong and dominating; it no longer carries burdens because it is weak like a young calf. The spirit now dominates and the soul follows along like a little calf following its mother.

As we look at the third living creature, we need to examine a number not yet seen in our Ezekiel study. Bullinger says concerning three:

Three stands for that which is solid, real, substantial, complete and entire.

All things that are especially complete are stamped with this number three.

God's attributes are three: omniscience, omnipresence, and omnipotence.

There are three great divisions completing time— past, present, and future.

Three persons, in grammar, express and include all the relationships of mankind.

Thought, word, and deed, complete the sum of human capability.

Three degrees of comparison complete our knowledge of qualities

Three kingdoms embrace our ideas of matter—mineral, vegetable, and animal.

When we turn to the Scriptures, this completion becomes Divine, and marks Divine completeness or perfection.

The number three…must be taken as the number of Divine fullness. It signifies and represents the Holy Spirit as taking of the things of Christ and making them real and solid in our experience.

The third day was the day on which the earth was caused to rise up out of the water, symbolical of that resurrection life which we have in Christ… Hence three is a number of Resurrection, for it was on the third day that Jesus rose again from the dead. (Bullinger 1967, 107)

Bullinger's book contains 16 pages on the number three. The portions quoted above will suffice for our understanding of this Revelation passage.

The number three, or rather third, tells us these mature Christians are now complete in Christ. This is why they can be seen in heaven. They have endured the cross and are living resurrection life in union with Christ. They have the face of a man and because the calf indicates they still have their earthly soul, the portion that has not yet passed into spirit, they are still on earth. We must remember that soul is defined as "the animal sentient principle only" and is distinguished from the "rational and immortal soul." They are able to enter this dimension of heavenly experience because the soul is completely in submission to the spirit.

The fourth living creature reveals more fully that they are still on earth and yet able to be in heaven at the same time. We have seen the number four many times in our study thus far.

The number four always has reference to all that is created. It is emphatically the number of Creation; of man in his relation to the world as created. It is the number of things that have a beginning, of things that are made, of material things, and matter itself. (Bullinger 1967, 123)

So the fourth living creature confirms again that these beings are of the earth. The fact that "fourth" is used in connection with the "flying eagle," explains that while they are of the earth, they have also risen upon eagles' wings into the very throne room of God in heaven. They are positioned as Jesus was when he said, "And no man hath ascended up to heaven, but he that came down from heaven, even the Son of man which is in heaven." Rather than coming down from heaven as Jesus did, they are of the earth yet at the same time raised into heaven and are citizens of both places.

Chapter Twelve
Rising Above the Soul

Verse 21- The Mind Leads the Way

When those went, these went; and when those stood, these stood; and when those were lifted up from the earth, the wheels were lifted up over against them: for the spirit of the living creature was in the wheels.

There are no Hebrew words for "these" and "those" in this verse. Some translations such as the *New International Version* and the *New Living Translation* have interpreted this verse without these pronouns.

NIV – When the creatures moved, they also moved; when the creatures stood still, they also stood still; and when the creatures rose from the ground, the wheels rose along with them, because the spirit of the living creatures was in the wheels.

NLT – When the living beings moved, the wheels moved. When the living beings stopped, the wheels stopped. When the living beings flew into the air, the wheels rose up. For the spirit of the living beings was in the wheels.

Others chose to use the pronouns:

NKJ - When those went, these went; when those stood, these stood; and when those were lifted up from the earth, the wheels were lifted up together with them: for the spirit of the living creature was in the wheels.

NAS – Whenever those went, these went; and whenever those stood still, these stood still. And whenever those rose from the earth, the wheels rose close beside them; for the spirit of the living beings was in the wheels.

I have quoted these translations to show how much liberty translators often take in order to make sense of a difficult passage. Some added the words "creatures" or "living beings" where King James and others used "these" and "those," but none of these words are in the original Hebrew. Some translations make it appear that the wheels are following the creatures but that cannot be right because we have firmly established that "wheels" are minds. Obviously, our mind decides where we go and the rest of our being follows.

For our spiritual translation, I believe using the pronouns will help us come to a more accurate understanding of this passage as the Holy Spirit enlightens us as to their antecedents.

In verse 20 we learned that when the minds went, the spirits went, but there are other parts of us that need to rise up also. These would be the natural body and the spiritual body. When the living creatures are rising up, these are not left behind.

The second half of this verse is identical to the second half of the preceding verse:

...the wheels were lifted up over against them: for the spirit of the living creature was in the wheels. In the preceding verse these words were referring to the spirits and the minds being lifted up together because the spirits were within the minds. Therefore, we can assume that in verse 21 the first set of "those and these" must be referring back to the spirits and the minds of the preceding verse. When those went (when the minds went), these went (the spirits went).

This whole series of verses about the living creatures going someplace began back in verse 19 where the living creatures "went" and the living creatures were "lifted up." The Holy Spirit has been showing us about the different parts of these living creatures (persons) as they are lifted up. We tend to think of ourselves as being one whole unit. The Holy Spirit is giving us the details about our inner makeup concerning our individual parts so we will understand the changes taking place in us that enable us to rise up in the spirit into the presence of the Father in heaven.

Things that have been connected are being disconnected so we can rise up into the dimension of spirit called heaven. The thing that has held us earthbound is the soul. Watchman Nee teaches in his three-volume work, *The Spiritual Man*, that the soul is between the spirit and the body and connected to both. In verse 19 the spirit was lifted up above the soul. Here in verse 21, the body too will be lifted up above the soul's dominance. The body's connection with the soul has kept it subservient to self and the forces of self-preservation and propagation. As a result of the fall, these drives have ruled our body subjecting us to the law of sin and death. This law of death must be removed if we are to rise up into divine health and heavenly places with Christ. Paul talks about this law of sin and death in Romans 7 where he says:

> For we know that the law is spiritual: but I am carnal, sold under sin. For that which I do I allow not: for what I would, that do I not; but what I hate, that do I. If then I do that which I would not, I consent unto the law that it is good. Now then it is no more I that do it, but sin that dwelleth in me. For I know that in me (that is, in my flesh,) dwelleth no good thing: for to will is present with me; but how to perform that which is good I find not. For the good that I would I do not: but the evil which I would not, that I do. Now if I do that I would not, it is no more I that do it, but sin that dwelleth in me. I find then a law, that, when I would do good, evil is present with me. For I delight in the law of God after the inward man: But I see another law in my members, warring against the law of my mind, and bringing me into captivity to the law of sin which is in my members. O wretched man that I am! who shall deliver me from the body of this death? I thank God through Jesus Christ our Lord. So then with the mind I myself serve the law of God; but with the flesh the law of sin (Rom. 7:14-25).

As we come into God's fullness, he will remove the law of sin from our "members" (our physical bodies) and "deliver us from the body of death."

One night after a day of intense study of the four living creatures, God gave me a dream that helped me understand the separation of the two bodies and the removal of mortality from the physical body. In this dream my mother gave me a family heirloom—a coffee table that on the underneath side had the signatures of all my grandmothers from ages past. The coffee table had two levels that were connected one to the other on each side by some sort of hinge device that held them about six inches apart yet gave them mobility in that they could move back and forth independent of each other. At one point I saw myself holding one half of one level in my hands. I looked at the coffee table and it looked complete yet I had one half of one level in my hands that had been cut straight down the middle.

As I prayed for the interpretation of the dream, God revealed that the coffee table represented my natural and spiritual bodies as inherited from my ancestors. The bodies were separate yet connected and mobile. The half I held in my hands was the portion representing mortality that God had severed and removed. The coffee table was now complete but immortality had replaced the place where mortality had dwelt.

A few nights later my husband (who had not read this manuscript) also had a spiritual dream. He dreamed he was going to be operated on. The bottom half of his body was going to be removed and he was getting a new half. In the dream he was happy about having the operation—like there was no fear, only delightful anticipation. I believe the bottom half represented the mortality in his body that was going to be replaced with immortality.

Before stating our spiritual interpretation for verse 21, we need to look at two Hebrew words. First, the word translated as "stood," is 'amad which may also be translated as "arise." The second, "over against" is 'ummah, which according to Gesenius may also be translated as "in communion." All the different parts of the person are now in communion with one another. With the removal of sin, a new synergy exists amongst all parts of their being, enabling all parts to ascend with the exception of the natural soul (earth) that keeps them related to the physical realm of human life.

Here is our spiritual interpretation of verse 21 in its entirety:

When the minds went someplace, the spirits followed (When those went, these went). And when the minds and spirits arose (and when those stood), the bodies arose also (these stood). This was because they had risen above the soul (when those were lifted up from the earth). The minds (the wheels) were able to lift them all up because all parts were in communion with one another (were lifted up over against them). This is because the spirit of the person was in the minds (for the spirit of the living creature was in the wheels).

Verse 22- The Unused Portion of the Mind
And the likeness of the firmament upon the heads of the living creature was as the colour of the terrible crystal, stretched forth over their heads above.

At first glance one might think the firmament was "the color of a terrible crystal stretched forth over their heads above," but "firmament" is not the subject of the sentence but rather the object of the preposition "of." The subject of the sentence is "likeness" or "parables." This new language of parables seen as visions in the imagination of the mind is taking these persons into the very presence of God in a new dimension. As we examine each word starting with firmament, we will learn more about the inner working of God as he makes the necessary changes in us to enable us to enter fully into his presence.

The Firmament
The first place we find this word "firmament" is in the first few verses of Genesis 1:

And God said, Let there be a firmament in the midst of the waters, and let it divide the waters from the waters. And God made the firmament, and divided the waters which were under the firmament from the waters which were above the firmament: and it was so. And God called the firmament Heaven. And the evening and the morning were the second day (Gen. 1:6-8).

God called the firmament heaven. In the Old Testament, the word most often used for heaven is *shamayim*. According to *Holman's Bible Dictionary*, heaven could be described as a partition God made to separate the rain-producing heavenly waters from the rivers, seas, and oceans below.

This is an outward explanation but we need to remember that our entire interpretation of the four living creatures is about what is happening inwardly not outwardly. The Old Testament focused on outward rituals and forms while the New Testament reveals the inward reality of faith and the indwelling of Jesus Christ. Keeping this principle in mind, we can see that this partition or this firmament is within us and is separating waters above from waters below within our being. What are these waters? I believe Scripture will reveal these waters to be spiritual truth—a revelation of the one who said, "I am the way, the truth and the life."

To gain a better understanding about these waters, we need to go back to the Garden of Eden:

> And a river went out of Eden to water the garden; and from thence it was parted, and became into four heads. The name of the first is Pison: that is it which compasseth the whole land of Havilah, where there is gold;
>
> And the gold of that land is good: there is bdellium and the onyx stone.
>
> And the name of the second river is Gihon: the same is it that compasseth the whole land of Ethiopia. And the name of the third river is Hiddekel: that is it which goeth toward the east of Assyria. And the fourth river is Euphrates (Gen. 2:10-14).

Andrew Jukes in *Types in Genesis* explains that the river in the Garden of Eden that was only one stream is a type of living water...the truth of God in its entirety. Those of us on this side of the veil are not able to grasp truth in the vastness of this dimension. Therefore it comes to us in four different streams or rivers. The Pison River represents moral and spiritual truth we receive apart from our natural senses. Gihon is truth about material things received through our natural senses. Hiddekel, also called Tigris, represents truth that comes to us through the testimony of others concerning what they have learned via their intuition and senses. The last river, Euphrates, is a type of our process of reasoning whereby we assimilate what we have learned according to intuition, our natural senses and the testimony of others.

The river that was one stream as it watered the garden represents the full manifestation of Jesus Christ that one can expect to encounter in heaven. Until then, while on earth, we ascertain our knowledge of him on a limited basis as we learn about him through our intuition, perception, the testimony of others and reasoning.

Entering into the fullness of Christ will mean coming to the place where we are watered by that one stream in the garden as we come face to face with our Lord. This will entail passing across the firmament—that within us that separates us from this full revelation of Jesus Christ.

We will learn more about this firmament as we examine another Old Testament word for heaven, *galgal*. There is only one passage in Scripture where *galgal* is translated "heaven" although it is in the Bible eleven times. Nine times it is translated "wheel," one time it is translated "rolling" but only one time is it translated "heaven." The one verse where it is translated "heaven" is Ps. 77:18, "The voice of thy thunder was in the heaven" *(galgal)*. Here this word for heaven is associated with the voice of God from heaven.

We will be learning about a new development in these mature Christians (living creatures) where they are going to be hearing clear and distinct communication from the other side of the veil. In verse 24 of Ezekiel 1 we will examine words like "voice of the Almighty," "the voice of speech," "noise" and "a voice from the firmament that was over their heads."

Since *galgal* is translated "heaven" and also "wheel," and wheels, we have learned, are the mind, we have a direct connection between "firmament" and our mind.

Firmament = heaven = wheel = mind.

According to Gesenius, it was believed that the firmament of heaven was spread out "like a hemisphere above the earth, like a splendid and pellucid sapphire (Ex. 24:10, compare Dan. 12:3) to which the stars were supposed to be fixed, and over which the Hebrews believed there was a heavenly ocean."

A wheel (our mind) is an entire circle. A hemisphere (the firmament) is half a circle. This represents the half or portion of our minds that we don't use. It has long been known that we human beings only use part of our brain. Scientists and psychologists have long debated whether or not the mind is within the brain. Whether it is or is not is immaterial for our study here but if we only use part of our brain, and the scriptures are telling us here that we only use part of our mind, there must be some connection.

In this verse of Ezekiel, the likeness (parables) of the firmament "was stretched forth over their heads." It would seem logical that the thing stretched forth would be the firmament, but since parables are the subject of the sentence, they must be the things "stretched forth."

It is interesting to see how different translators have handled this verse:

There was a surface spread out above them like the sky. It sparkled like crystal (NLT).

Spread out above the heads of the living creatures was what looked like an expanse, sparkling like ice, and awesome (NIV).

Over the heads of the living creatures there was something like a dome, shining like crystal, spread out above their heads (NRSV).

Now over the heads of the living beings there was something like an expanse, like the awesome gleam of crystal, extended over their heads (NAS).

How differently KJV handles this verse:

And the likeness of the firmament upon the heads of the living creature was as the colour of the terrible crystal, stretched forth over their heads above.

Only in the KJV are we able to see the actual subject of the sentence as being "likeness." What God is going to be showing us here is that the parables seen as visions in the imagination of our mind are the vehicle God has made to transport us across the firmament (formerly unused portion of our mind) into heaven. As God takes us across via the parables, the parables will be coming from the unused part of our mind opening our understanding about things we have never before known. We will see this more fully when we examine the words, "color of the terrible crystal." However, before we do this, we have much more to learn about the firmament.

Since God called the firmament "heaven," we need to look at this word more closely in Strong's. Here is his definition for the most commonly used Hebrew word for heaven:

Heaven - 8064. shamayim, shaw-mah'-yim; dual of an unused sing. shameh, shaw-meh'; from an unused root mean. to be lofty; the sky (as aloft; the dual perh. alluding to the visible arch in which the clouds move, as well as to the higher ether where the celestial bodies revolve):—air, X astrologer, heaven (-s).

What we need to notice here is the duality of this definition. Heaven can be either the visible arch in which the clouds move or the higher ether where celestial bodies revolve. Here in Ezekiel, the firmament represents the part of our mind that we don't use that must be crossed in order to see into heaven. This part of our mind is covered with clouds (or partitions [veils]) blocking our view of the higher ether where God, the angels and the departed saints dwell (heaven).

We see in our Ezekiel passage the words "stretched forth." The Bible tells us in Isa. 51:13 that God "stretched forth the heavens." This word "stretched forth" is *natah*, a prime root meaning "to stretch or spread out," and "by implication to bend away." According to Webster, bend means "to turn or be turned from a straight line or from some direction or position."

As human beings, we can only see in straight lines—that is to say, we can't see around the bend. When I'm driving my automobile on a two-lane road and want to pass the car ahead of me, I can't do it when there is a bend in the road because I can't see if any oncoming traffic is on the other side. Heaven is bent to us. It is around the corner and we can't see or hear from heaven except in brief glimpses as God permits. The fact that I can't see or experience heaven doesn't mean it is far away. It just means there are limitations placed on my abilities in that I cannot see around corners. This is true geographically but also concerning time. I can't see what is ahead, around the bend, for my life except as revealed to me by the Holy Spirit. As the unused portion of our mind is activated, we will find a new ability to see around the bend and experience heaven.

Adam, while still in the garden, must have possessed a magnificent mind as evidenced by his ability to create a name for every living creature God made. He also had the ability to hear the voice of God—an ability that was lost as a result of the fall. Part of the curse pertains to our minds as seen in the labor we must exert in learning, memorizing, understanding, etc., and also in our inability to hear the heavenly voices.

We are seeing here in Ezekiel that God placed partitions in our minds (the firmament being a partition in our mind, viz. a part of our mind we no longer use) that block our accessibility to the vast abilities originally inherent in the mind of humankind. This is shown to us pictorially in the account of our forbearers being cast out of the garden.

In Revelation 22, heaven is described as being a garden. As we look back to the Genesis account where Adam and Eve were cast out of the garden, a type of heaven, we see that God placed barriers or partitions at the east of the garden to ensure that we could not enter back into the garden. These partitions are the cherubim and the flaming sword. In order for anyone to enter into the garden while still on this earth, they must first pass through the cherubim and the flaming sword.

The Cherubim

Understanding how we get back to the garden, a place where there was uninterrupted fellowship with God as "they heard the voice of the Lord God walking in the garden in the cool of the day," requires understanding the mystery of the cherubim. (The Hebrew word for "cool" is *ruwach*, most commonly translated "spirit" or "mind." Day can also mean "an age." We could say, they heard the voice of the Lord God walking in the garden in the spirit of their mind in a certain age.) To enter once more into the garden is not to say we will be like Adam and Eve before the fall because we will have a maturity they did not possess. However, we will have access to those things we lost as a result of the fall.

Let's examine a few things the Bible and others have written about these cherubim. Then we can combine all we've learned about cherubim with our revelation of the four living creatures and the Holy Spirit will reveal to us just exactly who these creatures are.

In Hebrews 9 where the Ark of the Covenant is described, we read, "and over it the cherubims of glory shadowing the mercyseat; of which we cannot now speak particularly." The fact that the Holy Spirit could not speak about them at that time suggests they concern secrets of the end times—things that could not be known until now. Solving the mystery of the cherubim over the mercy seat may require understanding the revelation of the four living creatures because one of the creatures' four faces, the face of an ox, changes to the face of a cherub in Ezekiel 10. This gives us a direct connection between the cherubim and human beings in the end times. Chapter 1 of Ezekiel shows the preparation of these human beings while Ezekiel 10 reveals their end time ministry. When they come into the fullness of Christ, they will no longer have the face of an ox, but the face of a cherub. We explained earlier that the ox represents the natural soul of man and that one of the stages of entering into Christ's fullness involves the natural soul being severed from the rest of our being and removed.

God's instructions for the making of the cherubim over the ark in Exodus 25 reveal several truths about these beings.

> And thou shalt make a mercy seat of pure gold: two cubits and a half shall be the length thereof, and a cubit and a half the breadth thereof. And thou shalt make two cherubims of gold, of beaten work shalt thou make them, in the two ends of the mercy seat. And make one cherub on the one end, and the other cherub on the other end: even of the mercy seat shall ye make the cherubims on the two ends thereof. And the cherubims shall stretch forth their wings on high, covering the mercy seat with their wings, and their faces shall look one to another; toward the mercy seat shall the faces of the cherubims be. And thou shalt put the mercy seat above upon the

ark; and in the ark thou shalt put the testimony that I shall give thee. And there I will meet with thee, and I will commune with thee from above the mercy seat, from between the two cherubims which are upon the ark of the testimony, of all things which I will give thee in commandment unto the children of Israel (Exo. 25:17-22).

The ark has long been considered a type of the Lord Jesus Christ. Many wonderful books have been written revealing the truths seen in this lovely Old Testament type, so we will concentrate mainly on the cherubim. The mercy seat that covered the ark is a symbol of Christ's atonement. In the New Testament the word used for mercyseat is *hilasterion* which is also translated "propitiation." The cherubim were made from the same piece of gold as the mercy seat suggesting they are rising up out of the atoning work and life of Christ. The atonement was for human beings, not angels. With the ark symbolizing Christ and the cherubim being one with it, we can only conclude they represent human beings. Angels in heaven can never become one with Christ. This is a privilege reserved for redeemed humanity.

The cherubim were made of pure gold. Gold represents the purity of the life of Christ. The gold was beaten representing the suffering of these beings. Leaving the cherubim as depicted over the mercyseat for a moment, let's look at a few more things written about them and then come back and finish this.

Strong defines the cherubim as being "imaginary figures." This connects the cherubim with the imagination.

God spoke to Moses from between the cherubim on the mercy seat; therefore, we can conclude that cherubim have something to do with hearing the voice of God. "And when Moses was gone into the tabernacle of the congregation to speak with him, then he heard the voice of one speaking unto him from off the mercy seat that was upon the ark of testimony, from between the two cherubims: and he spake unto him" (Num. 7:89).

The Scriptures tell us in seven places that God "dwelleth between the cherubims" (1 Sam. 4:4; 2 Sam. 6:2; 2 Kings 19:15; 1 Chron. 13:6; Ps. 80:1; Isa. 37:16; and Ps. 99:1), and yet, we know God's dwelling place is with man.

Jesus Christ did not take on human flesh, suffer an agonizing death on the cross and be resurrected in order to dwell with some heavenly order of angels as some have believed cherubim to be. He did all this because he wanted to dwell in humankind. He is Emmanuel, God with us. He dwells within us. This again connects the cherubim with human beings. However, Strong's definition of cherubim is "imaginary figures." How can all this be reconciled? The answer is that the cherubim are symbolic of parables seen as visions in the imagination. We come into God's presence and hear his voice speaking to us as we come to him via the parables in our minds.

There are two cherubim rising up out of the mercy seat with the mercy seat being the atoning work of Christ. One of these is Christ as seen in the imagination. The other represents the individual having the visions. They are both made of beaten gold because both have suffered death. Jesus, of course, died for us and we in turn must die to self and everything of this world in order to come into his image. Both are pure gold as both are without sin. This is how we are to see ourselves in the parables—sinless and perfected in the image of Christ.

They "stretch forth their wings on high, covering the mercy seat with their wings" (Ex. 25:20). The Hebrew word for "covering," cakak, means "to entwine as a screen" and "to protect." "Wings" are still the imagination. In the making of parables seen as visions in the imagination, the imagination of the person is combined with the imagination of Christ much as the materials of a screen are woven together. These parables provide protection for the persons and bring them into the fullness of all Christ died for. The cherubim seen as protecting the ark itself are interpreted spiritually as the parables of the imagination guarding and bringing to full salvation these individuals. As we continue envisioning ourselves in relationship with Jesus in heavenly places, we will rise up into the full realization of his atoning work for us.

Continuing in Ex. 25:20 we read, "and their faces shall look one to another; toward the mercy seat shall the faces of the cherubims be." This reveals that in the parables we are looking into the face of Christ and his face, as always, is turned toward ours. At the same time, we are looking at many aspects of the atonement by personalizing his love for us via the parables. It is here God speaks to us. It is here we are able to perceive his love and closeness in ways never before known.

As we stated previously, the only way one could enter back into the garden (paradise) would be to pass through the cherubim and the flaming sword. As we envision ourselves with Jesus in the heavenly parables, we pass through the cherubim. The other obstacle, the flaming sword, tells us, I believe, the time frame for returning to the garden. The word "flaming" means "enchantment." "Enchantment" makes me think of spells or curses. Jesus is returning with a sword and with his return will come judgment and the lifting of the curse that has been on the earth and all living creatures since the fall. There is a sharp two-edged sword coming out of his mouth symbolic of the Word of God and we know from Heb. 4:12 that "...the word of God is quick, and powerful, and sharper than any twoedged sword, piercing even to the dividing asunder of soul and spirit, and of the joints and marrow, and is a discerner of the thoughts and intents of the heart." Only as Jesus wields his sword on us will we be able to enter into paradise.

Having established that the subject of this verse is the parables and that the firmament is the unused part of our mind, we can examine the next word, "heads." One definition for head, ro'sh, is "beginning." Now we can say that...

The parables (and the likeness) from the unused portion of the mind (of the firmament) were beginning something in these mature Christians (upon the heads).

The next words, "was as the color of a terrible crystal" reveals what was beginning. Color, 'ayin, can also be translated "knowledge."

Terrible, yare', according to Gesenius also means "wonderful" and "reverence." Reverence involves having a sense of awe about something. At this point our spiritual interpretation reads:

The parables (and the likeness) from the unused portion of the mind (of the firmament) were beginning in these mature Christians (upon the heads) a knowledge (was the color) that was exceedingly wonderful and awesome (of a terrible).

The Unused Portion of the Mind is Spiritual

That which was "terrible" or exceedingly wonderful and awesome concerns the word "crystal." Our study of crystal will reveal that the unused portion of our mind is actually spiritual in nature. Verses 20 and 21 revealed that the spirit was in the mind. Verse 22 is telling us that this spirit comprises the firmament—the unused part of the mind. This part of the mind, once it has been awakened by God, will be able to comprehend spiritual truths far beyond anything we have ever known.

Crystal, qerach, means "ice (as if bald, i.e. smooth)". As we look at two Old Testament types, we will see that smooth means spiritual. The first concerns Jacob and Esau. In type they have long been recognized as spirituality (Jacob) and carnality (Esau). Most Christians remember Esau as being a hairy man—so hairy that when Jacob went in to deceive blind Isaac, he had to cover his hands and the smooth of his neck with skins of goats to convince him he was Esau. Perhaps few would remember a statement Jacob made prior to this deception when he said to his mother Rebecca, "Behold, Esau my brother is a hairy man, and I am a smooth man." Since Jacob represents that which is spiritual, ice which is described as smooth refers to spirituality.

Our second example of smooth and hairy concerns Elijah and Elisha. Elijah was noted as being a hairy man, "He was an hairy man, and girt with a girdle of leather about his loins" (2 Kings 1:8). James describes him as being a man "subject to like passions as we are" (James 5:17). Although God worked mighty miracles through Elijah, he sometimes reacted to unfavorable circumstances with unspiritual behavior and attitudes. When Jezebel threatened his life, he ran into the wilderness and asked to die (fear, self-pity). Then he lamented that he was the only one in Israel who had remained faithful to God (pride). Clearly Elijah, a hairy man, although a mighty prophet of God, was sometimes very carnal.

Not so with Elisha who was a bald, or smooth, man. He seemed to be above the carnal human emotions demonstrated by Elijah. The miracles wrought by Elisha were more diverse and numerous than Elijah's and these miracles did not end with his death. When a dead man was thrown into Elisha's grave and touched his bones, "he revived, and stood up on his feet" (2 Kings 13:21).

These Old Testament types reveal that the word "crystal" shows the unused portion of the mind is spiritual in nature. It also discloses why it has been inactive—it is ice. Spirit is sometimes analogous to water in scripture. Jesus said to the woman at the well, "...whosoever drinketh of the water that I shall give him shall never thirst; but the water that I shall give him shall be in him a well of water springing up into everlasting life." When water is frozen, the water in inactive. Water from a frozen well would be inaccessible.

This crystal is "stretched forth." "Stretched forth," *natah*, can also mean "unfolded" according to Gesenius. Webster explains unfold as, "to open and spread out," "to make known or lay open to view, esp. in stages or little by little," "reveal" "to develop fully."

This unused portion of our mind that is spiritual in nature is gradually unfolded by God. It is made known to us in stages as, little by little, God opens it and reveals more of himself to us. Our ability to perceive spiritual realities is gradually developed until we come into fullness.

Our spiritual interpretation of verse 22 now reads:

The parables (and the likeness) from the unused portion of the mind (of the firmament) were beginning in these mature Christians (upon the heads) a knowledge (was the color) that was exceedingly wonderful and awesome (of the terrible) from the formerly unused portion of the mind that was spiritual in nature that had been frozen or inaccessible but was now being opened and revealed little by little by God (crystal, stretched forth over their heads above).

The last phrase of this verse is, "over their heads above."

"Over," *'al*, also means "above."

"Heads," here will mean intelligence and reason because according to Webster, the head is "the seat of reason, memory, and imagination;" "mind;" and "intelligence."

Above, *'alah*, may also be translated "high."

These words reveal that the knowledge these mature Christians are beginning to experience as the spiritual portion of their mind is awakened and unfolded is...

far above (over) all human reason, memory, imagination or intelligence (their heads) because it was coming from on high (above).

Our entire spiritual interpretation for verse 22 reads as follows:

The parables (and the likeness) from the unused portion of the mind (of the firmament) were beginning in these mature Christians (upon the heads) a knowledge (was the color) that was exceedingly wonderful and awesome (of a terrible) from the formerly unused portion of the mind that was spiritual in nature that had been frozen or inaccessible but was now being opened and revealed little by little by God. This knowledge was far above (over) all human reason, memory, imagination or intelligence (their heads) because it was coming from on high (above).

It is important to note here that as these mature Christians are having this experience with God, they are daily studying the Bible. All truth must be in accordance with the written Word of God. As the veils are removed and the unused portion of the mind is awakened, the Scriptures are opened before them in a depth never before revealed. Their personal experiences with God are in accordance to what they are seeing in the written Word.

My Experience

Over the years as Brenda has given me words from the Lord, he has many times said, "tonight I am going to remove a partition from your mind as I awaken more of your spiritual mind." I have learned that while we are sleeping, our God who never sleeps is working in us in ways we are not aware of. However, one night after he said he was removing a partition from my mind, I actually felt it happening just after I went to bed. I can't really explain the feeling except to say it was across my forehead and it was a pleasant feeling of something being peeled away.

The Lord has never said I need to visualize this taking place, but he has given me a picture of my spiritual mind being like honeycomb. I believe this concept of honeycomb can be confirmed in the account of Saul's son Jonathan who ate honeycomb and the result was that his eyes were enlightened. "But Jonathan...put forth the end of the rod that was in his hand, and dipped it in an honeycomb, and put his hand to his mouth; and his eyes were enlightened" (1 Sam 14:27). Of course, the eyes being enlightened here would be spiritual eyes.

Chapter Thirteen
New Realms in God

Verse 23 - New Health for the Natural Body
And under the firmament were their wings straight, the one toward the other: every one had two, which covered on this side, and every one had two, which covered on that side, their bodies.

This verse will show how the opening of the unused portion of the mind that is spiritual in nature affects these mature Christians. We again encounter the word "bodies" in this verse, and as we shall see, this verse is showing us that the opening of the unused portion of the mind affects the bodies.

This verse seems to be stamped with the number two. First we see it in the words, "one to another." Then again in "everyone had two." Also in the words "on this side" and "on that side," indicating there are two sides. We stated previously that "two" may mean there is a difference and that one is higher than the other. The word "under," *tachath*, also suggests there are two because, according to Gesenius, it can mean "the lower part." If there is a lower part, there must be a corresponding higher part. It also means "depressed," and "humbled." This refers to the natural body. It is the lower part, with the spiritual body being the upper part. This lower part is "under the firmament" or humbled and in submission to the now awakened formerly unused portion of the mind. In other words, this newly activated portion of the mind has an effect on the natural, physical body that is now in subjection to it.

"Wings" are still the imagination.

"Straight," *yashar*, means "to be straight or even; fig. to be or make right, pleasant, prosperous, direct, fit, to bring or make straight or be upright."

This verse shows that by using the imagination, the natural body, in subjection to the newly activated spiritual mind, is becoming right, prosperous, pleasant, fit, etc. In other words, it is being healed and delivered from the effects of aging and all that has not been right with the body. The activation of this portion of the mind gives far greater power to the imagination than it has had previously, and now these mature Christians are being raised into even higher dimensions of health and supernatural living.

"Under the firmament were their wings straight," means:

The natural body (Under) that was now submitted to the formerly unused portion of the mind that is spiritual in nature (the firmament) was becoming free from all sickness and the effects of aging (straight). This was being accomplished by God as the persons joined in the work with him by using their imagination (wings) that was now far more powerful because of the unfolding of this new portion of the mind.

The next words, "one toward the other," reveal more about what is taking place with the bodies. "Toward," *'el,* means "denoting motion towards." Earlier in the revelation of the four living creatures, God separated the natural body from the spiritual body in order to awaken the spiritual body and remove sin from the natural body, but the work has been accomplished and now it is time for the two bodies to come together into one glorious new body. Therefore one body is in motion towards the other.

"One toward the other," means:

One body (One) was moving towards (toward) the other body (the other).

The next words will explain more about what happens as these bodies begin to come together.

every one had two, which covered on this side, and every one had two, which covered on that side, their bodies.

"Two," means there is a difference and one is higher than the other.

"Every one," *'iysh*, occurs twice. It can also mean "each one." Once it refers to the higher part and once it refers to the lower part.

"Covered," *kacah*, means "to fill up the hollows." The word "hollow" suggests an empty space that needs to be filled.

Our spiritual interpretation for *every one had two, which covered on this side, and every one had two, which covered on that side, their bodies* is as follows:

As the two bodies were coming together, the upper part or spiritual body (everyone had two) was filling up the hollows in the lower part, the natural body, (which covered on this side) and the lower part or natural body (everyone had two) was filling up the hollows in the higher part, the spiritual body (which covered on that side, their bodies).

In order to fulfill God's purpose for his church in these end times, we will need to have a new body—a body that can interact with people and things on earth but at the same time can also move in the supernatural dimension of heavenly existence. The natural body as it is now is limited to the narrow confines of earthly time and space (something is lacking—hollows). Our eyes don't see into the dimension of heaven that is all around us. We are not able to walk on water or suddenly appear in a roomful of people without having walked through the door. Conversely, the spiritual body is not able to interact with solid objects. For example, a spiritual body cannot pick up a glass of water and hand it to a human being dying of thirst in a desert. Should a spiritual hand try to reach out and stroke a fevered brow, it would not be felt.

As the spiritual body and the natural body come together, each will fill in the hollows in the other. The resulting unified body will have the ability to simultaneously participate fully in two dimensions of existence that have hitherto been separated. As things stand now, those who are on earth do not have access to those in heaven until they shed their mortal body through death and pass into heaven. Those in heaven who at this time only possess a spiritual body are not able to interact with those of us still on earth. As we come into perfection spiritually by dying to self and walking in holiness, God will begin a work in our mind and body that will deliver us from death and transport us into a whole new dimension of eternal life while we are still on earth!

Our spiritual interpretation for verse 23 is as follows:

The natural body (Under) that was now submitted to the formerly unused portion of the mind that is spiritual in nature (the firmament) was becoming free from all sickness and the effects of aging (straight). This was being accomplished by God as the persons joined in the work with him by using their imagination (were their wings) that was now far more powerful because of the unfolding of this new portion of the mind. One body (One) was moving towards (toward) the other body (the other). As the two bodies were coming together, the upper part or spiritual body (everyone had two) was filling up the hollows in the lower part, the natural body, (which covered on this side) and the lower part or natural body (everyone had two) was filling up the hollows in the higher part, the spiritual body (which covered on that side, their bodies).

My Experience

I shared in an earlier chapter that immediately after my spiritual body was awakened, I could feel the Lord separating my spiritual body from my natural body. That was thirteen years ago. God has been doing a work in each body prior to bringing them together again. God has been removing sin nature from the natural body and bringing it under the control of the spiritual mind. The spiritual body has been maturing since it was first awakened. This awakening is much like a new birth. At first the Lord's touch was very slight and could only be perceived when I was being very still. But as the spiritual body has matured, his touch has become much stronger.

I asked the Lord if I am to visualize the two bodies coming together. His answer was, No. I can understand that because it would not be relational. I would be focusing on myself rather than Jesus. He has shown me a different way to visualize as I will explain below.

That unforgettable moment when I felt my spiritual body awakening was on February 11, 1997. Five days later on my birthday I had an amazing experience that lasted for about 12 hours…an experience I have not had since. I was ministering to Brenda one evening in the church office when I began to realize that I felt that Jesus and I were one. My hands looked like his hands and mine at the same time. My feet looked like his feet, but they also looked like my feet. This is difficult to describe because it was totally supernatural. The sensation lasted for the rest of the night but was gone the next morning.

I believe this was a prophetic experience. I believe I was feeling something that we can expect to experience when we come into the fullness of Christ. There will be times when we are ministering that we will experience this feeling. At that time we will know that the things that come into our mind are not our own thoughts but God's. He may direct us to give a word of knowledge, prophecy, etc., and when we are experiencing this oneness, we will know that it is straight from God and not of ourselves. There may be other times when we will feel this. Maybe we will feel it all the time. I don't know for sure, but it is a wonderful feeling and one I want to have again.

Lately on my daily walks with Jesus, he has instructed me to imagine that we are one as I walk. I form a mental image of Christ in me and of myself in Christ. The New Testament tells us we are to put on Christ. I do that literally as I visualize this oneness. I picture my feet resting upon his feet as we walk. I visualize his legs strengthening mine. I see his head coming over mine…his brain over my brain, his eyes over mine, etc. I have been doing this for several weeks. I have noticed that I have more strength when climbing up the steep hills. I have more energy for the rest of the day. I have less desire to snack or overeat, and I am warmer (a great benefit in western New York in the winter)! I have been walking regularly for years but there is definitely a difference in the way I feel since I have been visualizing this oneness.

Verse 24 - Hearing the Voice of God

And when they went, I heard the noise of their wings, like the noise of great waters, as the voice of the Almighty, the voice of speech, as the noise of an host: when they stood, they let down their wings.

Now that the bodies are coming together and thereby filling up that which was lacking in each dimension, a new level of the imagination is activated. Until now the main focus of the imagination has been visual as parables were seen pictorially in the mind. Now sound is being added.

The word "noise," *qowl,* is the same word as "voice," and is seen five times in this one verse, again in the following verse and again in the last verse for a total of seven, the number of perfection and completion. This repetition signifies something very significant is happening here. The voice is first in the imagination but by the end of this verse, the persons will have let down their wings. The imagination will no longer be needed for hearing because they will actually be hearing the voices of heaven. However, the imagination will never be discarded, as it is part of our having been made in the image of God. It is from the imagination that creativity flows, and ministry in the end times will be marked by great creativity and many parables because we will minister in much the same way Jesus ministered.

The voice may not be heard with the ears of the body. It may be heard in the heart. I have had only one experience with hearing the actual voice of God. It came about fifteen years ago. I was asleep when I heard very clearly a distinctly male voice call my name. I awoke instantly but never heard it again. It was as clear as any voice I have ever heard, but I knew I had not heard it with my natural ears. I had heard it in the region of my heart. I knew it was the voice of God.

First he hears a voice speaking in his imagination (I heard the noise of their wings). As he continues imagining the voice of God, a passageway into the very presence and actual voice of God begins to open before him (like the noise of great waters).

Ps. 77:19 states, "Thy way is in the sea, and thy path in the great waters, and thy footsteps are not known." This word "path," *shabiyl,* means "a passageway (as if flowing along)." The spiritual mind that was frozen and inaccessible has now melted and become flowing waters carrying this person into God's presence. He is being led through the passageway of the formerly unused portion of his mind.

Next he hears "as the voice of the Almighty." He is hearing a voice that sounds like the voice of God. According to Andrew

Jukes in his book, *The Names of God,* this particular name for God, "Almighty," is usually *El Shaddai,* but in this passage, *Shadday,* refers to God in his power to transform us by giving his life to us.

To be "Almighty," He must be able to carry out His own will and purpose to the uttermost. And this will is to save His creatures, and to restore and re-form His image in them. If He cannot do this, and "turn the hearts of the disobedient to the wisdom of the just," He is not able to fulfill the desire of His nature, and so would not be Almighty...And, because He is Love, to "subdue all things to Himself" is to subdue all things to Love. (Jukes, Chapter 3)

The following phrase, "the voice of speech," reveals that this voice comes faintly and indistinctly at first and then builds as seen in the Hebrew word for "speech," *hamullah.* There are eleven different Hebrew words that are translated "speech." If we examine the definition for each of these words, we find that the word used here, *hamullah,* is the only word that also means "tumult." This word occurs only two times in the Old Testament—here in this Ezekiel passage and again in Jer. 11:16 where it is translated "tumult." According to Webster, our English word "tumult" comes from the Latin, *tumultus,* meaning "swelling or surging up." This reveals that the voice of God begins softly or indistinctly and then gradually increases and becomes more distinct.

The phrase, "as the noise of an host," reveals that not only does he hear the voice of God, but also he hears other voices of the hosts of heaven. There are basically three Hebrew words translated as our English word "host." The word used here, *machaneh,* is different from the other two words in that it can mean "angels," "the sacred courts," or "stars."

We have seen in this verse that the ability to actually hear from heaven begins first with the imagination. By using the imagination, a passageway is opened through the formerly unused portion of the mind and soon the person begins to hear the voice of God. This voice begins softly or indistinctly but gradually progresses to the point that the person hears very clearly. Then he begins to hear the voices of angels, departed saints and the hosts of heaven.

What Will God Say?

This verse ends with the words "when they stood, they let down their wings." When Jesus heard the audible voice of God for the first time as recorded by Scripture, it was at the time of his baptism when God said, "This is my beloved Son in whom I am well pleased." God was affirming his Son in his identity with these words.

These are words we all need to hear from our heavenly Father. I believe that as God speaks to us in this new dimension, we will be hearing words of love, affirmation and acceptance. We only truly know who we are in Christ when we are able to hear him tell us who we are. (He has ways of telling us this without our hearing an audible voice, but when we hear his voice I believe this is what he will be telling us.) His words are always edifying and loving. His perfect love releases us to be all he has called us to be in him.

I do not yet hear God's audible voice; however, I have heard him many times through his prophets and most recently through the prophetic words and visions of my friend Brenda who began leading me through the veils into his presence back in 1996. Brenda has heard the audible voice of God, but the primary way she hears is like most of us do, in that still small voice. Her earliest words and visions for me were primarily about God's love for me. I hung on every word. No matter how much we have been loved in this life (and I have been blessed greatly with the love of family my entire life), we still need to hear God tell us of his love. I would read the prophecies and listen to the tapes over and over again until I had some of them memorized. I could never get enough of hearing God speak of his love for me.

It is by knowing how deeply loved we are, that we are able to stand in these end times. When we no longer doubt God's love for us, when we know that we are accepted by him and desired by him, we have the strength to withstand anything the enemy throws our way.

An important aspect of coming into the fullness of Christ has to do with learning to stand. As the book of Ephesians teaches us, we are first to recognize our position of being seated in heavenly places in Christ Jesus. As joint-heirs with Christ, we have been given his authority and the power to overcome all things in this life. Next we learn to walk in this position in Christ by the way we live according to God's Word and our relationship with him. Finally, we must stand. As Ephesians 6 states, "having done all...stand." This is a position of victory as we stand upright before God the Father, not bent towards any idols and undaunted by the barrage of attacks the enemy inevitably hurls against us.

We learn to stand primarily by being assailed by the enemy. As we learn to wield the weapons of warfare Christ has given us, (putting on the full armor [Eph. 6], the Scriptures, praise, love, unity of the brethren, etc.), we grow stronger in Spirit. Things that used to bring us down into hopelessness, fear and defeat no longer affect us. We learn who we are in Christ as we battle the Devil's lies and choose to accept God's truth until we arrive at the place of standing before the Father with our eyes solely upon him. In this position, all the enemy's assaults bounce off us in total failure. What I have stated here in two paragraphs may take many years or even a lifetime to achieve, but it is possible to come to this place of standing.

Jesus is our pattern. Immediately after his baptism he was driven by the Spirit into the wilderness where he was tempted by the Devil for forty days. At the end of that time, he came forth victorious and the Scripture says that he "returned in the power of the Spirit into Galilee."

As we are tried and tested we must remember that no matter how severe the attacks of the enemy become, we can overcome all things in Christ. As we learn to stand secure in the love of the Father, knowing who we are in Christ and having "walked the walk," our God will defeat all our enemies even as they are already defeated through Christ's perfect work.

Those who have learned to stand are experiencing their position of rest. They have walked out their earthly course, and now they are standing before God Almighty and the sacred courts of heaven. They are like Joseph, when after all the years of suffering and preparation he finally stood before Pharaoh and began his great ministry in Egypt. "And Joseph was thirty years old when he stood before Pharaoh king of Egypt" (Gen. 41:46).

Having reached this place of maturity and standing, they now "let down their wings." They no longer need the imagination in order to hear God and experience his love and fellowship. They are actually in heaven while still on earth.

Here is our spiritual interpretation of verse 24 in its entirety:

And as the mature Christians were continuing their progress towards God, (and when they went), they were hearing a voice in their imagination (I heard the noise of their wings). As they continued using their imagination to hear the voice of God, a passageway was opening before them through the formerly unused portion of their mind that was spiritual in nature (like the noise of great waters). They were beginning to hear the actual voice of God (as the voice of the Almighty). At first this voice was soft and difficult to understand, but gradually it became stronger and more distinct (the voice of speech). Not only were they hearing the voice of God, but they were also hearing the voices of the hosts of heaven (as the noise of an host). These Christians had come into full maturity and were standing in the presence of God (when they stood). Now they no longer needed to use their imagination to experience their relationship with God as they had arrived in heaven into the presence of God while still on earth (they let down their wings).

Verse 25 – The Passageway to Heaven Has Been Opened
And there was a voice from the firmament that was over their heads, when they stood, and had let down their wings.

The previous verse revealed that the persons having this experience are hearing the voice of God, a voice that is helping to transform them into the image of God. This subsequent verse establishes the location of the voice they are hearing. The voice is not coming from some distant place high in the sky but is actually coming from within themselves, from the other side of the unused portion of their mind that has been awakened by God. This formerly unused portion of the mind (firmament) is like a passageway that connects them with the spiritual dimension of heaven. By actively using their imagination in conjunction with the guidance of the Holy Spirit, this passageway has been opened. Now they are able to hear the voice of God and the voices of the hosts of heaven.

The last half of this verse states the fact that this is only possible because they have reached the mature position of standing. They have lived a life of sacrifice and obedience to God—they have "walked the walk," and God is bringing them into the final stages of the fullness of his Spirit.

And there was a voice from the firmament that was over their heads, when they stood, and had let down their wings, will be interpreted as meaning spiritually:

And there was a voice (And there was a voice) coming from the other side of the formerly unused portion of their mind. This part of their mind had become a passageway that led them to heaven, a place that was far above their own ability to reason, imagine, or understand by using their own intelligence (from the firmament that was over their heads). They were able to have this experience because of their mature walk of faith that had prepared them to be lifted up to this high place in God (when they stood). They were hearing the actual voice of God because they were no longer using their imagination (and had let down their wings).

Chapter Fourteen
In Heaven with God

Verse 26- the Parables Continue in Heaven

And above the firmament that was over their heads was the likeness of a throne, as the appearance of a sapphire stone: and upon the likeness of the throne was the likeness as the appearance of a man above upon it.

In this verse we see the words "likeness" and "appearance"—familiar words to us now as we have seen them many times prior to this in our study of the four living creatures. Parables (likeness) and visions (appearance) were things we saw in our imagination. However, these mature Christians have "let down their wings." At this point they are no longer using their imagination to envision the parables. They are actually seeing these things in heaven. Their spiritual body and their natural body are in process of coming together whereby that which is lacking in each dimension of their bodies will be filled. There is a new ability for these persons to see and hear spiritual realities—an ability that was not present before the bodies were uniting.

This verse is telling us what the voice in the previous verse is saying. The word "likeness" occurs three times in this one verse. The Holy Spirit wants to emphasize to us the way he desires to speak with his people. Jesus spoke in parables during his earthly ministry, and when we see him here in heaven, he is still speaking to us in this kingdom language. God's wisdom and love are so far above our understanding, that were he to speak to us in abstract terms, we would not understand. Were he to reveal himself to us as spirit without form, we could not fully relate to him. When I think of God as being omnipresent, I can only picture him like a mist that surrounds and covers the entire earth and extends out into the universe. I have difficulty relating to him in that imagined form. But when I think of him in his personal relationship with me, as fully God yet fully man, I can relate to him.

This verse is about a throne. God is conveying to the believer who has broken through to this place of revelation a message about the authority and power being entrusted to him. This communication could come in the form of words where God might say, "I am raising you up to a level of great power and authority for ministry in these end times." This statement would be factual and informational but not very relational. By communicating with us via story and vision, the same message becomes intimate and exciting, conveying the heart of God in an unforgettable way that transcends the limitations of mere language. Parable and vision take us beyond, "I am raising you up to a level of great power and authority for ministry in these end times," to...

Jesus scooped me up in his arms holding me close against his chest like a bridegroom carrying his bride across the threshold. As we looked deeply into each other's eyes, he carried me up the steps of a throne and sat down with me on his lap. I saw a twinkle of mirth in his eyes and suddenly he burst out laughing!

"Oh, my Beloved," he said. "I can see the hoards of hell shrinking back from you with their tails between their legs because of the power and authority of your ministry. When you walk into a room full of people, the demons will flee in terror before us. As we go forth together, no force in hell will be able to thwart the great things I intend to do through you. I have longed for this day when you would sit with me upon my throne even as I sat down with my Father upon his throne.

This second way of speaking is in the form of a story—a story that is relational and gives a picture that would not be easily forgotten. In this allegorical story we see God's desire for intimacy, the concept of bride and bridegroom, his joy and anticipation of seeing his people overcome the Devil and advance his kingdom on earth, the authority being given the believer, more about the character of God, his strength, etc. This way of communicating is far superior to mere words.

Now that the visions are coming directly from God without the aid of the imagination, a new depth of intimacy is seen that would not have been possible just using the imagination. In our humanity, we would not be able to think of Jesus doing the things described above.

When Jesus ministered on earth, people did not understand his parables and many were offended, especially the religious leaders. It will be no different in these end times. The intimacy and personality of Jesus revealed above will be offensive to some people who have held him at arm's length and imprisoned him in ecclesiastical forms and theological dogma. Many use the words "bride" and "bridegroom" but are offended at the suggestion of any closeness beyond bowing at Jesus' feet. He is high and lifted up and seated upon the throne of all power and authority, but in his love he longs to hold us close to his breast and relate with us in ways we can understand. It will take all of eternity to explore the depths of his great love. A man who loves this deeply, even though he is God, wants close, intimate relationships and expressions of that intimacy with his people. Jesus would not say, "I love you so much I died for you, but don't touch me, or kiss me or sit close to me." Sometimes we allow our own sense of shame and our misunderstanding to separate us from a closer relationship with our Lord.

We have established that verse 26 is about God speaking in an allegorical vision to an overcomer about the authority and power being given to him/her for their great end time ministry. John, the one who penned God's message to the churches in Revelation, immediately after writing that overcomers would sit with Jesus on a throne, was caught up into heaven and given a vision of a throne. There are many similarities between John's account and our Ezekiel passage, and one of these is that the first thing seen in heaven is a throne. We will confirm, as we finish our Ezekiel 1 study, that John is seeing the overcomer and Jesus seated together on the throne. In Ezek. 1:20, we established that the four living creatures of Revelation 4 are the same four living creatures seen in Ezekiel's vision. In Revelation, these four living creatures are in the midst of the throne and round about the throne. They represent the overcomers in their position of authority with Jesus but at the same time around the throne at his feet in worship. In our study of Ezek. 1:27, we will more thoroughly identify the one seated on the throne.

Here in Ezek. 1:26, the "likeness of a throne" is "as the appearance of a sapphire stone." The sapphire stone is going to reveal something about the power and authority being given to the mature Christians. Our understanding of the sapphire stone will come from Exodus 24 where God called the leaders of Israel to Mount Sinai to worship him.

> Then went up Moses, and Aaron, Nadab, and Abihu, and seventy of the elders of Israel: And they saw the God of Israel: and there was under his feet as it were a paved work of a sapphire stone...(Exo. 24:9, 10)

The first thing we notice about the sapphire stone is that it is under his feet. This phrase "as the appearance of a sapphire stone" reveals that the power and authority being given to these mature Christians (throne) is on the basis of their being under his feet, totally under the authority of Christ.

> But every man in his own order: Christ the firstfruits; afterward they that are Christ's at his coming. Then cometh the end, when he shall have delivered up the kingdom to God, even the Father; when he shall have put down all rule and all authority and power. For he must reign, till he hath put all enemies under his feet. The last enemy that shall be destroyed is death. For he hath put all things under his feet. But when he saith all things are put under him, it is manifest that he is excepted, which did put all things under him. And when all things shall be subdued unto him, then shall the Son also himself be subject unto him that put all things under him, that God may be all in all (1 Cor. 15:23-28).

These mature Christians (four living creatures) are the first to enter into the fullness of Christ at the end of the age at the time of his return. For them, the last enemy, death, has been destroyed. In their individual lives, all things are now under his feet. They will minister with great authority because they are under authority.

If we examine the places in Scripture where the sapphire stone is mentioned, we can see that it does, indeed, refer to believers. The sapphire was one of the stones in the breastplate Aaron wore over his chest. Each stone represented one of the tribes of Israel—God's people.

In Song of Solomon where the Bridegroom is described, we read, "his belly is as bright ivory overlaid with sapphires." The belly refers to the heart. "Bright ivory," would be perfect whiteness denoting the purity of his heart. "Overlaid" tells us the sapphire stones, representing his people, are over his heart. His love for us is perfect and pure, and he keeps us as close to himself as possible—over his heart of pure love.

Approximately 90-95% of all sapphire is heated. Gems have been heated for over 4,000 years. Indian gem dealers discovered gems improved with fire. The old method, which is still used today, involves putting rough or finished gems in a crucible. This process involves no science, gauges, meters, timing, or control. Basically, the stones are put inside a steel drum. The drum is open at the top. Fire bricks line the bottom of the tank, leaving a circular opening from top to bottom. The fire is ignited with kindling and charcoal, then the crucible is inserted. The stones are cooked overnight. Other cookers utilize electronic furnaces and computers. They use chemistry, engineering, physics, and magic. They bathe the gems in oxygen, hydrogen, and cycle the gems with precise digital increments. Every cooker has his own theories and secrets. By using this alchemy, they make brownish sapphires blue and black sapphires blue. One thing to remember is that heating sapphire is a permanent process. Sapphires have all the right internal chemistry inherent in the crystals. They just were not in the earth's surface long enough, or were not located in exactly the right hot spot of the earth's crust to arrange the atoms properly. (http://www.preciousgemstones.com/gf winterpartone.html Accessed May 8, 2008)

This process should sound all too familiar to one who has seriously followed after God. There is only one way to be conformed to his image and that is to allow him to put us in a crucible and take us through the fire that we may be purified. In the process everything black or brown in us (contaminated by sin) will become blue (heavenly). Those who are sapphire stones are those who have known the suffering that comes with laying down one's own life in order that Christ may live in them. They have embraced the fellowship of his sufferings and allowed all things in their life to be under his lordship thus enabling them to be very close to Jesus, next to his heart. These are the ones who can fully identify with the purification process a natural sapphire endures.

Looking once more at Exodus 24, where they saw the God of Israel, there was under his feet a paved work of a sapphire stone. "Paved," *libnâh*, means "whiteness," (a type of holiness) and "by implication transparency," (having nothing to hide) which describes the condition of believers lifted up as in Ezekiel One. So this throne, in appearance as a sapphire stone, reveals that the power and authority given to these mature Christians (throne) is given on the basis of the purity and holiness in their lives wrought through their suffering and the work of God that has enabled them to submit totally to the lordship and authority of Christ.

Here is our spiritual interpretation of verse 26 in its entirety:

On the other side of the formerly unused portion of their mind (And above the firmament), they hear God speaking about things that are far above all human understanding, reason or intellect (that was over their heads). In order for them to fully comprehend, God speaks in the form of a parable (was the likeness). He is telling them about the power and authority being entrusted to them (of a throne). Not only are they hearing God's voice but they are seeing visions of heaven (as the appearance). God explains he is able to place them in this position of power and authority because they have been willing to die to everything in their lives (of a sapphire stone). This parable about their authority (and upon the likeness of the throne) is seen as a story in the form of a vision (was the likeness as the appearance) in which they see a man upon the throne (of a man above upon it).

More about Power and Authority

Those of us living in these ends times will come up against the greatest evil of all time. Think of all the atrocities of bygone years and then multiply that times a hundred and it will not be as bad as what is about to erupt full force on earth. The evil that the media reports daily is only the tip of the iceberg. However, this is as God said it would be. But along with his warnings of evil, he also tells of the power and glory of his people that will be manifested at that time.

"Arise, shine; for thy light is come, and the glory of the LORD is risen upon thee. For, behold, the darkness shall cover the earth, and gross darkness the people: but the LORD shall arise upon thee, and his glory shall be seen upon thee. And the Gentiles shall come to thy light, and kings to the brightness of thy rising" (Isa 60:1-3). This passage is said by some to be referring to the Jews, but others see it as the church...spiritual Israel. Matthew Henry says of this passage, "Darkness shall cover the earth; but, though it be gross darkness, darkness that might be felt, like that of Egypt, that shall overspread the people, yet the church, like Goshen, shall have light at the same time."

"The Lord shall arise upon thee." That is what we are learning about in the four living creatures. God is preparing us for his glory! This glory will be visible. People will recognize that God is within us and they will come to us because they will have had their fill of darkness.

The Bible promises that "...the earth shall be filled with the knowledge of the glory of the LORD, as the waters cover the sea." As the light and the glory of the Lord come upon his people in the end times, a ministry will go forth such as the world has never seen. We will do the "greater works" Jesus spoke of in John 14. As we are changed, we will encourage others and help them come into the fullness of God. They in turn will help others. It will grow exponentially and we will go forth into all the earth.

Remember the vision that Sue Anne had in chapter one? She saw that people would look at those who were perfect and burn up. This was not a literal burning up of the people. It was a picture of sin in them being burned up. This great end time ministry will have to do with judging the church. We will be able to see into people and tell them what is within that they need to repent of. As they repent and turn to God, the sin will be burned up in the judging fires of God. And if they don't repent, there will be the burning judgment of God upon them for their refusal of his Word.

We see some of this ministry in the chapters immediately following Ezekiel One. Ezekiel is sent forth to the children of Israel (a type of the church) who, the Lord says, are stubborn and rebellious. The Lord says whether they hear and obey or whether they resist your words, they will know that a prophet has been among them. This ministry will be prophetic with the ability to see within people and give specific words from God to help them change.

In Ezekiel chapter three is the well known passage stating that if we fail to warn someone and they die in their iniquity, their blood will be upon our hands. This shows that those who minister in this level of power and authority will be held to a higher standard of accountability than we have known in the past. This is because these end time ministers will not be wondering whether they heard from God or if it was just their own thoughts. They will hear clearly from God and their failure to obey will cause powerful consequences. The more of God's power and glory we are given, the greater our accountability before God will be.

Verse 27- The New Man
And I saw as the colour of amber, as the appearance of fire round about within it, from the appearance of his loins even upward, and from the appearance of his loins even downward, I saw as it were the appearance of fire, and it had brightness round about.

This verse will explain that the man seated upon the throne is the New Man.

...put on the new man, which after God is created in righteousness and true holiness (Eph. 4:24).

... ye have put off the old man with his deeds; and have put on the new man, which is renewed in knowledge after the image of him that created him (Col. 3:9b,10).

The person is seeing him/herself perfected and joined with Christ—not as two separate individuals, but as one person. He/she is now in the image of Christ and united with him in holy matrimony. This is what Paul speaks of in Ephesians 5:

...we are members of his body, of his flesh, and of his bones. For this cause shall a man leave his father and mother, and shall be joined unto his wife, and they two shall be one flesh. This is a great mystery: but I speak concerning Christ and the church.

What I am about to say may be offensive to some people, but we must remember our verse here in Ezekiel is revealing a spiritual reality. We are given a picture, something we can see and associate with life as we know it, to convey a deep, spiritual truth. Verse 27 of our Ezekiel passage gives us a picture of the bride and the Bridegroom as one flesh, joined together as husband and wife for eternity. "From his loins even upward," speaks of Christ. "From his loins even downward," is the believer. The loins are the place of procreative power, the place where a man and woman become one flesh in marriage. This is not to say there is an actual physical, sexual union between the believer and Christ, but that they are joined together in one body in the most intimate relationship possible between two persons. Christ is the upper part, and he will forever be the One who is high and lifted up with all power and authority. The believer is the lower part in complete subjection to and adoration of the One above her—the picture of a perfect marriage.

John saw this New Man in Revelation 4, "...behold, a throne was set in heaven, and one sat on the throne. And he that sat was to look upon like a jasper and a sardine stone..." The jasper stone is the believer and the sardine stone is Christ.

Jasper was the last stone in Aaron's breastplate. With each stone representing one of the tribes of Israel, or typically believers, the last stone, if we view them chronologically, would be those believers on earth in the end times. He who is last shall be first. They were born last but they will enter into Christ's fullness first. The jasper stone was on the fourth row—the number four tying it in with the four living creatures and with earth although it is seen in heaven.

The bride of Christ is likened to a jasper stone in Revelation 21 where the angel said to John, "Come hither, I will show thee the bride, the Lamb's wife. And he carried me away in the spirit to a great and high mountain, and showed me that great city, the holy Jerusalem, descending out of heaven from God, having the glory of God: and her light was like unto a stone most precious, even like a jasper stone, clear as crystal." A precious stone shines most brilliantly when there are no occlusions or dark spots to block the flow of light through the stone. These "jasper" believers, without spot or wrinkle, have no sin left to hinder the flow of Christ's life and light through them. The walls of this great city were made of jasper—these are support walls that uphold the structure signifying the great ministry to the body of Christ that will come forth in the end times through these mature believers.

The sardine stone is seen nowhere else in all of Scripture. The only thing we know about it is that it is red. This signifies Jesus, the one who shed his blood for us, Jesus the Great Redeemer, Jesus in his love for all of humanity, and because of this great love, he has seated on the throne with him, the overcomers. Hence John saw one seated on the throne like a jasper and a sardine stone.

Now that we have established who is on the throne, we need to return to the beginning of our verse to complete our spiritual interpretation.

And I saw as the colour of amber, as the appearance of fire round about within it... The fire here is the glory of God that is seen in and through this New Man.

"Color," *'ayin*, also means "sight" or "knowledge."

Amber is a precious stone consisting of translucent fossil resin that is yellowish to brownish in color. It can be highly polished and was used by the ancients in a variety of ways but chiefly for jewelry. The most precious amber is the most clear. Some amber is opaque because of minuscule oxygen bubbles trapped within the resin. Amber that was exposed to heating by the sun's rays had the surface weakened so that the tiny bubbles of oxygen could leave thereby resulting in a very clear and precious stone. We are like clear amber when we submit our lives to Jesus, our Sun. When the hindrances of our lives that block our view of Jesus are removed, we are able to see clearly in ever deepening levels of truth and revelation.

The middle of this verse has already been explained. For the remaining clause, "and it had brightness round about," we will return to our original definition of brightness taken from Webster, "the luminous aspect of a color (as distinct from its hue) by which it is regarded as approaching the maximum luminance of pure white or the lack of luminance of pure black." This believer has gone through judgment and the sin nature has been removed from his life. He has become pure white. He will never be as God in his glorious omnipotence, omnipresence and omniscience, but in character he is now like Jesus, and Jesus can flow out from him in miraculous manifestations of God's power and love even as he did when he was on earth in human form 2000 years ago. He will again be on earth but in a many-membered body that is in total subjection to the Father.

The life of Jesus is the pattern for our own lives. In these end times, we should expect to have a transformation experience similar to what Peter, James and John witnessed of Jesus on the Mount of Transfiguration.

(He) was transfigured before them: and his face did shine as the sun, and his raiment was white as the light (Matt. 17:2).

...he was transfigured before them. And his raiment became shining, exceeding white as snow; so as no fuller on earth can white them (Mark 9:2,3).

the fashion of his countenance was altered, and his raiment was white and glistering (Luke 9:29b).

I believe that in the midst of the suffering and confusion at the end of this age, when the fullness of God's judgment comes upon the earth, there will be those who will actually appear in the same type of visible transformation witnessed by the three disciples. Here in our Ezekiel passage, however, he is seeing a vision of himself not intended at this point for others, but for his own information.

Our spiritual interpretation of verse 27 follows:

And I saw with sight and knowledge that was clear (And I saw as the colour of amber), a vision of the glory of God all around and within the one on the throne (as the appearance of fire round about within it). In this vision I saw myself joined with Christ in the mystery of spiritual marriage alluded to by Paul in Ephesians 5. Christ was the upper part and I was the lower part (from the appearance of his loins even upward, and from the appearance of his loins even downward). I saw a vision of the glory of God (I saw as it were the appearance of fire) in the New Man who had become perfected and was now like Christ in character (and it had brightness round about).

Verse 28 – Perfection Has Come

As the appearance of the bow that is in the cloud in the day of rain, so was the appearance of the brightness round about. This was the appearance of the likeness of the glory of the LORD. And when I saw it, I fell upon my face, and I heard a voice of one that spake.

Ezekiel 2:1 And he said unto me, Son of man...

The previous verse reveals there is no more darkness, no spot of sin left in this person. He/she is like Christ in character, and because of this, verse 28 tells us there is no more judgment necessary in this individual's life. As with Noah, the rainbow signifies the end of judgment.

The cloud is the cloud that brings the latter rain. "In the light of the king's countenance is life; and his favour is as a cloud of the latter rain" (Prov. 16:15). God's favor is upon this life because this person has the countenance of Jesus. Now God can pour out his blessings without limitation because there is no need for further judgment. Sin has been dealt a deathblow and the light of Christ shines forth unhindered from this person's life.

James tells us, "Be patient therefore, brethren, unto the coming of the Lord. Behold, the husbandman waiteth for the precious fruit of the earth, and hath long patience for it, until he receive the early and latter rain. Be ye also patient; stablish your hearts: for the coming of the Lord draweth nigh" (5:7,8). It is time for the coming of the Lord. He is pouring himself into this person continually like a long, soaking rain that fully saturates the ground and fills every crevice till it can hold no more.

Ezekiel has been seeing a vision of God's plans to bring the church of the end times into his fullness and perfection. In this verse, as in the previous, we will speak of Ezekiel as the one experiencing this transformation because he is an Old Testament type of one having this experience.

As the appearance of the bow that is in the cloud in the day of rain, so was the appearance of the brightness round about. This was the appearance of the likeness of the glory of the LORD. And when I saw it, I fell upon my face, and I heard a voice of one that spake.

Our spiritual interpretation of verse 28 is as follows:

I was seeing in a vision (as the appearance) that my judgment had come to an end (of the bow), and God's favor was being poured out upon me (that is in the cloud). He continually poured himself into me until I was saturated with his Spirit, and yet he continued to come down upon me like the rains before the harvest (in the day of rain). I was shown that this was happening because there was no longer any sin nature in me (so was the appearance of the brightness round about). This was the vision (This was the appearance) of the parable of the glory of the Lord coming upon me (of the likeness of the glory of the Lord). And when I saw it, I fell down in total adoration and amazement (And when I saw it, I fell upon my face), at what God had accomplished in my life, and I heard the voice of the Lord speaking to me (and I heard a voice of one that spake), calling me by the same name he called himself, Son of Man...(Ezekiel 2:1 And he said unto me, son of man...).

Sue Anne's Vision Interpreted

Now that we have finished our study of Ezekiel 1, we have more understanding to apply to our interpretation of Sue Anne's vision in chapter one. The people she saw in the end times were absolutely perfect. They were the church without spot or wrinkle ministering in the power of God. They were also young. She had the vision in 1971. It is now 2010...39 years later. She was young when she had the vision. For her to look now as she did then would mean that the effects of aging were removed. Coming into perfection means that age will no longer be a factor. The four living creatures revealed how this will take place. When the sin nature has been removed, all the effects of sin's ravages on the body will be gone. We will have put off mortality and put on immortality.

She commented on demons being everywhere, hanging on the buildings and on the people. All the demons of hell are even now at work attempting to establish the reign of the Antichrist on earth and destroy every vestige of Christianity. When we reach perfection, we will see them. Nothing will be hidden from our spiritual sight. We will be able to see the spiritual causes behind people's actions and problems. No sin or deception will be able to hide from our eyes. We will have the power and authority to deal with the Devil and all his demons because we will have faced and conquered them on our way to coming into perfection in Christ.

Deliverance ministry will be very important in these end times. People have cast off the biblical restraints that used to undergird our society and in so doing have opened themselves up for demonic possession. The tremendous upsurge of interest in witchcraft and paranormal experiences also opens people to demonic oppression. Many of the most popular books and movies have themes based on the evil supernatural. People who avail themselves of these are picking up demons. At some point many of these people will realize they need deliverance and will turn to the church for help.

Another important part of this great end time ministry will involve administering the judgment of God. In the vision, the people who looked at those who were perfect burned up because they were being judged by God. They were either carnal Christians who were having all the sin nature burned out of them, or they were evil people who had rejected God and were being removed by God.

She saw people in the throne room with God who had what she called a "round shape" that was difficult to describe. I believe my brother was correct when he said those must have been people in their spiritual bodies. They may have been departed saints but they could also have been the end time ministers who were able to be with God in heaven even while they were on earth. This was revealed in the four living creatures.

She saw great darkness upon the earth. The sky, the earth, and the trees were all brown as though they had burned but they didn't really burn. The air was dirty and thick making it difficult to breathe. This may have been a description of spiritual darkness being over everything or extreme pollution or possibly the aftermath of a nuclear holocaust. To me it reveals how utterly and totally mankind has failed to take care of the beautiful earth entrusted to us by God.

There was one other thing said by Sue Anne that I did not include in the first chapter because it was so disturbing that I thought it needed to be interpreted in light of our completed study. She reported that God said he was going to operate on the world and the world wasn't going to live. We can take comfort in the promise found four places in Scripture that there will be a new heaven and a new earth.

Isa 65:17 For, behold, I create new heavens and a new earth: and the former shall not be remembered, nor come into mind.

Isa 66:22 For as the new heavens and the new earth, which I will make, shall remain before me, saith the LORD, so shall your seed and your name remain.

2 Pet 3:10 But the day of the Lord will come as a thief in the night; in the which the heavens shall pass away with a great noise, and the elements shall melt with fervent heat, the earth also and the works that are therein shall be burned up... 2 Pet 3:13 Nevertheless we, according to his promise, look for new heavens and a new earth, wherein dwelleth righteousness.

Rev 21:1 And I saw a new heaven and a new earth: for the first heaven and the first earth were passed away; and there was no more sea.

The only word Sue Anne could think of to describe God was "love" when she said "he looks like love." Love is also the predominant characteristic of God revealed in the four living creatures. Once the spiritual body has been awakened, one feels the Father's love 24/7. There is not one second of one day that this love is not felt. It is constant and gentle. The faithfulness of God is something we can actually feel along with the unchangeableness of his nature. It is permanent and enduring. No matter where we are or what we are doing, it remains the same. This love that was willing to leave its place in heaven, put on human flesh, suffer and die for us can now be felt in every molecule of our body. There are truly no words to describe the greatness and constancy of God's love.

We are living in the time spoken of in Daniel 12, "...many shall run to and fro, and knowledge shall be increased." Think of crowded airports and traffic jams. Put that together with the vast knowledge at our fingertips through the Internet. Can there be any doubt that we are living in that time spoken of in Daniel?

The adjacent verse says, "And they that be wise shall shine as the brightness of the firmament; and they that turn many to righteousness as the stars for ever and ever." Let us press on to know our God. Let us be like Jesus who turned his face like flint towards Jerusalem. Let us accept the cross of Christ and go on into perfection that we might be those who shine forth like the stars in the darkness of this evil age.

Works Cited

Bilson.
http://www.jeremiahproject.com/prophecy/signofthetimes.html.
Accessed Oct. 24, 2009

Bullinger, E. W. 1967. *Number in Scripture.* Grand Rapids:
Kregel Publications.

Chambers, Oswald. n.d. *My Utmost for His Highest.* New York:
Dodd, Mead & Co.

Clark, Glenn. 2001. "Seeing As Jesus Does." *Spirit Led Woman*,
June/July, 64-67.

DAN DEAN AND GARY SADLER, 2001 ARIOSE MUSIC,
FAVORITESONGS PUBLISHING, MEADOWGREEN
MUSIC COMPANY, PAINTBRUSH MUSIC, ASCAP,
ADMIN. BY EMI CHRISTIAN MUSIC PUBLISHING

Gesenius, H. W. F. 1979. *Gesenius' Hebrew-Chaldee Lexicon to
the Old Testament.* Grand Rapids: Baker Books.

Jukes, Andrew. 1976. *Types in Genesis.* Grand Rapids: Kregel
Publications. Originally published 1898. London: Longmans,
Green and Co.

Jukes, Andrew. *Names of God.*
http://alampthatburns.net/jukes/names/03-namesofgod-ch3.htm.
accessed Jan. 3, 2010.

Mulholland, M. Robert Jr. 2000. *Shaped by the Word.* Nashville:
Upper Room Books.

Nee, Watchman. 1965. *The Release of the Spirit.* Cloverdale:
Sure Foundation.

Payne, Leanne. 1985. *The Healing Presence.* Grand Rapids: Baker Books.

Strong, James. 2001. *The New Expanded Exhaustive Concordance of the Bible.* Nashville: Thomas Nelson Publishers.

CPSIA information can be obtained at www.ICGtesting.com
Printed in the USA
BVOW030158151111

276104BV00006B/1/P